BLESS THIS HOUSE

PRAYERS FOR FAMILIES AND CHILDREN

Gregory and Suzanne M. Wolfe

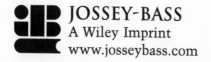

JOSSEY-BASS
A Wiley Imprint
www.josseybass.com

Published by Jossey-Bass
A Wiley Imprint
989 Market Street, San Francisco, CA 94103-1741   www.josseybass.com

Credits begin on page 213.

Jossey-Bass books and products are available through most bookstores. To contact Jossey-Bass
directly call our Customer Care Department within the U.S. at 800-956-7739, outside the U.S.
at 317-572-3986; or, fax 317-572-4002.

Jossey-Bass also publishes its books in a variety of electronic formats. Some content that
appears in print may not be available in electronic books.

Library of Congress Cataloging-in-Publication Data
Wolfe, Gregory.
  Bless this house : prayers for families and children / Gregory and Suzanne M. Wolfe.— 1st ed.
    p. cm.
  Includes bibliographical references and index.
  ISBN 0-7879-7297-5 (alk. paper)
  1. Family—Religious life. 2. Prayer. 3. Prayers. 4. Parenting—Religious aspects—Christianity.
  5. Christian education of children. I. Wolfe, Suzanne M. II. Title.
  BV200.W65 2004
  249—dc22   2004004603

Printed in the United States of America
FIRST EDITION
HB Printing 10 9 8 7 6 5 4 3 2 1

CONTENTS

For our children and yours

INTRODUCTION:
THE EARTHY SPIRITUALITY
OF FAMILY LIFE

Is there anything more pure, more full of wonder and hope for the future, than the prayer of a child? We find it difficult to imagine what that might be. For a child's heart, when it forms a prayer of thanks or praise or petition, has none of the self-consciousness and ambivalence of adulthood; it is a laser beam of light and love—focused, clear, and burning with urgency.

Prayer is natural to human beings, whether they are children or grown-ups. It takes place all the time, and not just in churches. As Rabbi H. H. Donin has pointed out, we pray even when we don't realize we're praying. "Thank God!" we sigh in relief, on hearing that someone we love is recovering from a serious illness and out of danger. Some prayers don't even invoke God's name: a gorgeous sunset might evoke a muttered response ("How glorious!") that is really an act of praise; a guilty conscience might bring us back to someone we've hurt ("Forgive me"), where our desire for reconciliation reaches upward as well as outward.

Each of these statements ultimately implies a hearer, which is why so many thinkers have defined prayer as a form of conversation, however one-sided it might seem at first sight. And a conversation is a form of communication between *persons*. The Christian tradition is grounded in the belief that our God is a personal God. There is nothing odd, then, when the great Metaphysical poet John Donne calls the blessed Trinity "three-personned" God. Children take the personal dimension of prayer for granted.

But prayer, like many other human capacities, will atrophy if it is not used and developed. A child possesses an innate ability to pray, just as he or she has a built-in capacity to learn language. No one would dream of being silent all the time around a child; we not only talk in the presence of our children, but we devote a great deal of time to teaching them words and their proper meanings, pronunciations, and grammatical relationships. As parents, we help our children learn to name and thus understand the world around them.

Prayer is a particular form of language (though it often aspires to go beyond words) that children can pick up with the same ease and facility that they do any kind of speech. But the tragic reality is that those of us who live in the prosperous Western nations have largely failed, in recent generations, to teach our children the language of prayer. The causes of this neglect are numerous—from a well-meaning but wrong-headed desire to allow children to shape their own young lives without parental intervention to sheer laziness. Exploring those causes is not within the scope of this book, but this much seems self-evident: to neglect children's spiritual lives is to impoverish them in some indefinable but real way.

YOUR CHILD'S SPIRITUAL
AND MORAL DEVELOPMENT

Christians have always known that children need to be trained in virtue. We believe that God's infinite goodness is the basis for morality. But the danger—even for the most fervent believer—is that morality comes to mean little more than a set of rules rather than a loving response to the God who first loves us.

In short, celebrating the virtues has rightly become an important element of character education, but too often discussion of the virtues remains abstract, as if discussions at home or Sunday school about courage will make children courageous. We do need to talk more about morality as a set of rules—children must learn the process of internalizing rules, after all—but the limitation of talk is that it remains a thing of the head and not the heart.

The secret to your child's moral and spiritual development is this: your child should not simply *admire* goodness but should actually *fall in love* with goodness. The Greek philosopher Plato believed that in order to live a full human existence, we must develop a feeling of *eros* for the Good. Today we associate the word *eros* with "erotic," or merely sexual, love, but for the Greeks, *eros* conveyed a passion that involved the whole of a person's character. In the Bible, God is frequently described as a lover who woos us.

Traditionally, it was in reading—and listening to—stories, including the great epic tales of heroes, that children developed *eros* for the good, the truth, and the beautiful. Storytelling anchors the virtues in the concrete experience of believable characters. Through the miracle of imagination, a child can enter into a sympathetic relationship with the heroes of great literature, vicariously experiencing both their mistakes and their achievements. In previous books, we have written on the relationship between storytelling and virtue, stressing the need to expose children to books and films that exemplify what we call the "moral imagination."

But in addition to storytelling, there is another path to a child's moral development—prayer. Prayer is a vital means through which children make the connection between virtuous behavior and their own emotional and personal growth.

For most of us, this is easier said than done. When approaching the question of praying with our children, the first problem we come to is often . . . ourselves. Our own prayer life may not be regular or fervent or rewarding. And so we are tempted to ask, "How can I teach my kids to pray if I don't know how to pray myself?" There's the rub. It's at this point where many of us hesitate, perched on the knife edge between good intentions and the challenge of putting them into practice.

We may feel we know the rudiments of prayer, but most of that knowledge relates to praying in church or in the silence of one's own heart. Praying aloud as a family involves a steeper learning curve than we might care to admit.

The notion of praying together as a family can seem at once embarrassing and intimidating, but it is just at this crossroads, this moment of hesitation, that grace lies in wait for us. When parents hesitate to teach children something they don't know themselves, they have already stepped out onto the right path, though they don't often recognize it. Most of us sense that prayer is something that we must practice before we can preach it. This desire to avoid hypocrisy is in itself a step in the direction of spiritual authenticity. In the life of the spirit, wanting is often the same as having. The twentieth-century French novelist Georges Bernanos once said, "The wish to pray is a prayer in itself. God can ask no more than that of us." And fifteen hundred years ago, Saint Augustine observed, "We would not seek You if we had not already found You."

And that brings us to the purpose of this book. It is our hope that we can provide encouragement—and a little help with the learning curve—as you embark on the adventure of praying with your children.

Of course, it is possible to purchase one of the dozens of collections of prayers for children on the market and give it to your children. But that would be a little like giving a two-year-old a dictionary and wishing her luck.

The central thesis of this book is that parents need to do more than simply give their kids prayers to say. Rather, parents themselves should learn to pray by praying *with* and *for* their children. While it is crucial that parents allow children to develop their own spirituality and to pray in their own words, the parent's participation adds a whole extra dimension. If we step outside the circle of prayer, we convey the message to our children that they are merely performing a duty. But when we enter that circle ourselves, we forge deep spiritual and emotional bonds with our children.

This leads directly to the other conviction at the core of this book: that there is nothing wrong with making family prayer the springboard that helps you develop your own interior life. The first thing that attentive parents discover when they teach their children to pray is that the children quickly become the teachers, reminding us of the innocence and wonder that we have lost and restoring it to us with a grace and simplicity that can sometimes take our breath away.

SACRED TIME

It's at this point that you might be thinking, But *when* can a family find the time to pray together? With music lessons, soccer games, and parents rushing off to evening PTA meetings, we're lucky if we even eat dinner together. Fair enough. But prayer is one of those things that we need to make time for, even if it is just before the kids get sent off to bed and we collapse into a comfortable chair. Prayer cannot stop time, but it can allow us to step into a different sort of time. When we cease our normal "worldly" activities to pray, we move from the horizontal to the vertical dimension. Instead of driving forward, we look "up." The theologians and mystics speak of worship as "sacred time." When prayer becomes a daily part of life, those moments of devotion seem to be linked together, almost as if prayer is a special *place* in our lives. That is the paradox of sacred time, that it puts us into a mode of existence that is simultaneously *set apart* and yet, in a mysterious way, truly our *home*.

Another way of putting the paradox is that when we look up to heaven, we are able to delight more fully in our life on earth. Saying grace before a meal makes that meal taste better. Does that sound odd or irreverent? It shouldn't. If we pray with real gratitude before a meal, we slow down just a bit and remind ourselves that every meal, however humble and quickly consumed, is a feast. A grace that our kids occasionally blurt out is "Good food, good meat, good God, let's eat!" The very speed of the prayer acknowledges our hunger, and yet even this jokey grace constitutes a tip of the hat to God, the giver of every good thing.

Just as we can help create pockets of sacred time amid the hurtling pace of daily life, so we can discover the way that prayer turns ordinary things into extraordinary things. When thinking about spirituality, the first mistake that most people make is to assume that the sacred exists on some transcendent plane that is remote from daily life. But you don't have to go to monasteries on mountaintops to draw close to God. In the Gospels, Jesus is always hallowing the most mundane of events, from meals to washing to visiting friends. If we are to encounter the sacred, we must find it in the mundane routines of eating and drinking, waking and sleeping, traveling and resting.

In a similar fashion, prayer should be understood not so much as a retreat from the ordinary as it is a hallowing, or consecrating, of the ordinary. A sacred space is built out of the same materials as any other building. And the holiest rituals of the world's faiths all center on the most mundane need of all—our need to eat. To break bread as a family is always an opportunity to consecrate the material goods we need for our bodies to a higher purpose—the love that ought to bind us closer to one another. We think it's safe to say that if you cannot glimpse the sacred in a simple family meal, you will not be able to find it on mountaintops or in deserts.

REAL FAMILIES, REAL PRAYER

In writing *Bless This House*, we have tried to produce something that is more than just a manual of prayer. We've taken a few tentative steps in the direction of what we can only call the spirituality of family life. In the course of assembling this book, we found—to our amazement—that very little has been written about the relationship between the ordinary, everyday experiences of living together as a family and the inner world of the spirit. Our emphasis, then, is not simply on the "how-to" of prayer but also on the moral and emotional *contexts* in which family prayer can take place.

Prayer is not a subject on which we consider ourselves authorities. Neither of us is ordained, nor do we have degrees in theology. In fact, we joked at one point about whether to title this book (with an eye to our own situation) *Prayer for Dummies* or *The Complete Idiot's Guide to Prayer.*

Our credentials for writing on this subject are simply that we are the parents of four children ranging in age from eight to nineteen and that we have been praying as a family for nearly two decades. In putting this volume together, we've relied on our own experiences, a few good books, and a series of conversations with spiritual writers who have plumbed the depths of prayer.

In short, we're not going to pretend that we're a Superfamily—clean-cut, well-adjusted, full of greeting-card sentiments. Not at all. We snap at each other when we're tired; we try—and fail—to balance work and family time; we struggle on a daily basis with selfishness, resentment, and anxiety. To put it delicately: we are an *expressive* family, which sometimes means that all six of us are expressing ourselves in very loud voices. On the other hand, we are also a physically demonstrative bunch—hugging, kissing, biting, wrestling, and so on. For better or worse, no emotion is repressed in the Wolfe household. And yet somehow we manage to hang in there, find the time to calm down, and even to lift our voices in prayer. Slowly but surely, prayer has become an essential part of our cohesiveness as a family.

It is all too easy, when addressing the subject of children and prayer, to slip into sentimentality and a pious, other-worldly tone—what the writer Patricia Hampl calls the "eau de cologne language of spirituality." We've tried to avoid that mind-set like the plague it is. On the contrary, we'd like to think of ourselves as "spiritual realists." As every parent knows quite well, family life is an exercise in barely contained chaos: babies crying, older kids rampaging, parents struggling with exhaustion and a day that is never long enough. Family prayer times are commonly beset by fidgeting, bickering kids, ringing phones, and distractions galore. In these circumstances, it doesn't seem likely that we will find mystical illumination or even emotional uplift.

That's why it is so important to remember that prayer is an art. Like any art form, prayer requires us to overcome the powerful forces of inertia. The life of the spirit requires time and discipline to grow; you can't just take a few prayers, add water, and expect instant holiness. The self-help industry has generated a lot of revenue by promising some quasi-sacred number of "easy steps" to healing, wisdom, and prosperity. To be honest, we feel that too many Christians have bought into the pop psychology of the self-help movement. The great spiritual masters know that the only effective steps are the small ones that we take every day of our lives—just like a one-year-old learning to walk.

The good news is that with discipline comes liberation. The obvious analogy here is with the musician who practices.

After practicing innumerable scales and arpeggios, musicians can play with such freedom that they seem to be making up the music as they go along.

So it is with prayer. Somehow, by placing ourselves on a daily basis in the precincts of grace, the joy of heaven can suddenly irrupt into our lives. In our household, there are times when family prayers take place in the midst of giggles, good-natured wrestling matches, and the occasional naughty joke. Our family would certainly scandalize those who think that piety requires a long face and rigid posture. But there's no reason why prayer has to turn anyone into a prig. Many of the great saints and holy ones have possessed a mischievous sense of humor. In this regard, Saint Francis springs to mind; he often indulged in playful irony. To take just one example, he loved to call his body, with all its embarrassments and complaints, "Brother Ass."

We've tried to write about prayer in the same vein of earthy humor and realism that characterized Saint Francis's approach to life. If prayer means anything at all, it is about the way the divine penetrates the earthly, making ordinary things radiant and turning the chaos of our days into a joyful dance. As G. K. Chesterton once said, "Angels fly because they take themselves lightly."

THE BREADTH OF CHRISTIAN TRADITION

There are other challenges that face those who attempt to write about prayer. For example, this book is addressed to a large and diverse Christian readership, and yet prayer is a practice that often takes place within specific denominations and traditions. What makes this even more difficult for us is that we have great respect for the differences and specific habits and rituals of the different sectors of the Christian communion. In compiling this book, we were faced with the question of how to show respect for specific traditions while also striving for breadth and variety in approaches.

In struggling to find the proper balance, we have followed two basic principles. First, both the selections of prayers and our commentaries on them keep to the middle of the stream rather than paddling up the individual tributaries. In other words, we include many prayers from the Roman Catholic tradition, but not the rosary or other prayers that involve a theology that is obviously controversial for non-Catholics. And so on.

Second, we've borrowed an idea from C. S. Lewis's popular book *Mere Christianity*. In his preface to that book, Lewis says that his exposition of Christian doctrine is intended to serve as a hallway—a meeting place where many different believers find common ground. But Lewis goes on to say that a hallway is not a dwelling place. Most of us need to find the door of the particular tradition that seems most welcoming to our spirits and then to enter into that room to eat our meals and get warm by the fire. Our hope is that this book will also serve as a hallway and that you will move on into the rooms where you can find nourishment and comfort.

PRAYING TO A PERSONAL GOD

Then there is the vital question of who it is that we are praying *to*. Some people would say that it doesn't matter to whom prayers are addressed because they have a therapeutic value in and of themselves. Prayer, to this way of thinking, has a calming effect and is simply a form of "personal expression." There's an element of truth to that. Prayer can bring deep inner peace, and it is always colored by our unique personalities. But we think that it is both ill-advised and self-defeating to think of prayer as merely a therapeutic device. If you approach prayer from a purely pragmatic point of view, as a kind of stress-relieving technique, you're bound to be disappointed. There are many practices, ancient and modern, that are geared to calming body and soul, including meditation, deep breathing, and guided visualization. Prayer, however, requires us to *speak,* and even if we never hear an audible answer to our prayers, the whole process makes sense only if we are entering into a conversation *with someone.*

Here the witness of our children can infuse a healthy dose of common sense into the discussion. A child addresses his prayers to a *person* and seeks attention—and answers—from that transcendent figure. Children have a startling capacity for praying in a naturally conversational tone, as if they were talking to a beloved aunt or uncle. Modern psychology has brought much good to our world, but some of its more ideological strains have tended to caricature faith and spirituality as the result of "childish delusion." We prefer to side with the Pulitzer Prize–winning child psychiatrist Robert Coles, who refuses to reduce faith to wish fulfillment. After a lifetime of work with children all over the world, Coles wrote *The Spiritual Life of Children,* in which he concluded that he sees children "as seekers, as young pilgrims well aware that life is a finite journey and as anxious to make sense of it as those of us who are farther along in the time allotted us."

We don't want to imply that prayer is incompatible with doubt or uncertainty about the existence and character of God. As most of the great spiritual writers attest, doubt is a close cousin to faith; healthy doubt, allied to an open mind and a curious heart, provides fertile ground for the inner life. Perhaps Coles's analogy of the pilgrim is apt here. A pilgrim is not a mere wanderer; he has a goal, whether that be God or some form of enlightenment. But even the most ardent pilgrim knows that he is still on the road, that the journey itself is marked by moments where the path is sometimes clear and sometimes hard to discern. Just be careful that you don't let your adult uncertainties become a burden to your child. And by the same token, don't assume that your child's faith is merely naïve, that it cannot help you recapture an intuitive knowledge that you've found it difficult to hold on to.

Jesus rebuked his disciples for keeping children away from him. They had fallen into a trap not unlike that of some psychologists: they looked on spirituality as the serious business of grown-ups. But Jesus said, "Let the children come unto me, and do not hinder them; for to such belongs the kingdom of heaven" (Matthew 19:14).

So with children as our guides and teachers, we write from the perspective that prayer is addressed to a personal God who created the world and who knows and loves each and every one of us in that world and who answers our prayers in real, if mysterious, ways.

HOW TO USE THIS BOOK

We have tried to design this book to make it as useful as possible. If you can, read it straight through to discover the entire gamut of prayers that we have included, as well as our thoughts and experiences with them. Then you can return to the book for daily or occasional prayers as best suits your family's habits.

The two initial chapters of *Bless This House* address the central features of prayer in the context of family life. The first focuses on the role that prayer can play in your child's moral, cognitive, and spiritual development. The second responds to the many practical questions that occur to parents when seeking to introduce their children to prayer. When do I begin praying with my children? What if parents are of mixed faiths? Are there particular places or postures that are conducive to prayer?

The remainder of the book is devoted to a collection of classic and contemporary prayers. Each section of prayers is introduced with anecdotes from our own family or others and contains practical suggestions for how to integrate the many different types of prayer into your family devotions. The prayers in each section always begin with selections that are geared to younger children and become progressively more mature. Many of the prayers may strike you as being too demanding for a young child. Some of them undoubtedly are. But we happen to believe that the greater danger is of condescending to our children. Prayers that are overly cute, sentimental, or simplistic don't have the resonance and mystery to draw a child deeper into the life of the spirit.

How did we go about selecting the prayers? Our criteria were straightforward. We looked for prayers from every corner of the globe and a range of Christian traditions. We also wanted examples of as many different types and occasions of prayer as possible. Finally, we wanted prayers that were substantial enough to be said again and again without becoming thin or trite. Since many hymn lyrics and poems have a powerful devotional dimension, we have not hesitated to treat these as prayers.

Our quotations from the Bible come from two classic translations—the King James Bible and the recent and widely acclaimed New Revised Standard Version. The poetry of the King James Bible has never been matched and is something that every child should hear, even if it isn't the translation that satisfies you for everyday use.

With the beauty and wisdom of these prayers to inspire you, perhaps you will be motivated to try writing some of your own.

It is our earnest hope that you will unlock your child's—and your own—potential for the divine conversation that is prayer. It is a well-known paradox of the spiritual life that when we gather together and focus our love and attention outward—on God's goodness and grace—we actually grow closer to one another. That is the secret of praying together as a family.

And now, instead of wishing you luck, we'll send you off into the adventure of prayer with a somewhat more spiritual and decidedly old-fashioned word:

Godspeed.

He prayest best, who loveth best
All things both great and small;
For the dear God who loveth us,
He made and loveth all.

SAMUEL TAYLOR COLERIDGE

HOW and WHY WE PRAY

~

The Soul in Paraphrase

STAGES IN YOUR CHILD'S PRAYER LIFE (AND YOURS)

There is a paradox at the heart of a child's spiritual life that often goes unresolved, and it is this: in order for a child to experience the fullest growth, parents need to make the first move. It's true that children can develop a profound spirituality even without help from their parents and even in the most dysfunctional and adverse circumstances. But the responsibility for nurturing the souls of our children rests squarely with parents. Just as children's educational performance and moral behavior depend to a great extent on the quality of their home life, so does children's progress in the realm of the spirit. If the school health class is no substitute for talking to your children about sex, why should anyone imagine that Sunday school is sufficient to nourish a child's spirituality?

OVERCOMING OBSTACLES TO PRAYER

To make prayer a living part of family life, there are two major hurdles that most of us have to get over. The first is a lingering sense that to pray with our children is somehow to impose something on them—the legacy of past generations' myths about freedom and self-determination. The second is the feeling that we are spiritually inadequate, that we cannot nurture our children's inner life because our own is not good enough. It's only natural to feel that these hurdles are impossibly high, that to leap over them will end in an embarrassing fall. But like so many things that we fear, we tend to make them larger and more ominous than they really are. Because both of these hurdles are based on misconceptions.

In *The Book of Virtues,* William Bennett responds to the notion that we don't have the right to impose our values on others by quoting an anecdote told by the nineteenth-century poet Samuel Taylor Coleridge. In Coleridge's day, the English freethinker John Thelwall had written that it was "unfair to influence a child's mind by inculcating any opinions before it should have come to years of discretion, and be able to choose for itself." When Thelwall later paid a visit to Coleridge's cottage, the poet took him outside. "I showed [Thelwall] my garden and told him it was my botanical garden. 'How so?' said he, 'it is covered with weeds.'—'Oh,' I replied, '*that* is only because it has not yet come to its age of discretion and choice. The weeds, you see, have taken the liberty to grow, and I thought it unfair in me to prejudice the soil towards roses and strawberries.'"

If we pray with our children in a spirit of love, there is little or no chance that they will be traumatized, even if they choose not to share all of our convictions when they grow up. Do we resent our parents simply because as adults our politics or our choice of profession is different from theirs? Only if parents exercise a spirit of coercion can prayer or any aspect of faith become a source of injury. But the very spirit of prayer is opposed to coercion. Children's hearts, to return to Coleridge's metaphor, are like soil that only needs weeding and planting; the soil itself gives the growth.

Of course, it's true that many children will resist the introduction of prayer into their lives. Kids are fairly conservative; they like routines and resist change. But it is vital that we distinguish between getting over a child's initial resistance to a new practice and the danger of parents becoming overbearing and coercive.

There is a right way and a wrong way to introduce prayer into family life, and it would be wrong for us to ignore the dangers of the wrong way. In researching this book, we've come across people who had negative childhood experiences with family prayer. We've talked to some people who hated "family devotions" when they were children, not because they were rebelling against religion, but because they felt excluded—that they were simply bored spectators rather than participants. "When I was a kid," our friend Jeanne told us, "we had family devotions after dinner. First we read from the Bible; then each of us kneeled down by our chairs while the parents prayed. My favorite possession during those years was a Cinderella watch, which I took apart so I could study the moving gears while everyone else closed his or her eyes. Back then, I think I associated prayer with a mechanistic universe."

Prayers become mechanical when a child feels cut off from what is going on around her. That's why our focus in this book is on the need for parents and children to pray together, to make prayer a shared adventure. As with so many habits and disciplines, prayer is easier to introduce when a child is quite young. Anyone who has prayed with small children knows that they need only the barest hint about what prayer is before they demonstrate a natural proficiency in talking to God. Teaching young children to pray is more like unlocking a gate than it is of imposing an alien point of view. In the next chapter, we deal more directly with the issue of a child's resistance to prayer and the challenges of introducing prayer to older children.

The more serious obstacle to praying with our children is our own sense of spiritual insufficiency. "How can I give my children what I don't possess myself?" At some point nearly every parent asks this question, consciously or unconsciously. There's a sound instinct at the heart of that question, but it can also serve as an excuse. If you postpone praying until your motives are pure and you've become an expert in theology, you'll never begin to pray.

The Christian writer Richard Foster, in his book *Prayer: Finding the Heart's True Home,* addresses the issue of the mixed motives we bring to prayer:

> The truth of the matter is, we all come to prayer with a tangled mass of motives—altruistic *and* selfish, merciful *and* hateful, loving *and* bitter. Frankly, this side of eternity we will *never* unravel the good from the bad, the pure from the impure. But what I have come to see is that God is big enough to receive us with all our mixture. We do not have to be bright, or

pure, or filled with faith, or anything. That is what grace means, and not only are we saved by grace, we live by it as well. And we pray by it.

In the Introduction, we quoted Georges Bernanos to the effect that the desire to pray is already a prayer. Perhaps that's evidence of the grace that Foster describes.

The notion that we need to possess a theological education before we can pray is another misplaced concern. The glory of prayer is that it accommodates almost any kind of human expression, from a single word ("Help!") to the most erudite composition of a religious sage. Prayer is not a sequence of words or pious thoughts; it is the act of opening one's heart to God. In our fear and insecurity, we think that we are unworthy, incapable of uttering the right words. But what does that say of our concept of God? Jesus says, "Come unto me, all you who are burdened, and I will give you rest." The yoke of Christ is light because he is shouldering it with us.

There is a wise old saying that "faith follows action." This means that we often have to act on our faith before we can feel the emotional reality of that faith. To use an image straight out of pop culture, we have to become like Indiana Jones in his quest for the Holy Grail: we have to step out into what sometimes seems like an infinite abyss in the hope that our feet will find solid ground. Prayer is the single most effective action that we can take to live out our faith, to bring that faith to life.

The faith that comes so naturally to children can renew our spiritual life. Living in faith is, after all, the very essence of childhood. Nearly every aspect of a child's life requires faith—a trust that food, shelter, clothing, and love will always be there. Children are utterly dependent on their parents, but unless they are living in an abusive situation, children wear this dependence lightly and even joyfully. Paradoxical as it might seem, children have an amazing capacity for *confident dependence,* which is perhaps the most concise definition of faith we know. In that sense, children are very close in spirit to the "lilies of the field" about which Christ speaks.

The tragedy of the fallen world in which we live is that somewhere along the line, we lose that sense of confident dependence. At some point, we seek to live out of our own will, to become masters of our own destinies. The result is fear, insecurity, and a restless heart. That's why praying with our children can become such a powerful source of personal, spiritual renewal. To pray with our kids, to nurture their spiritual lives and witness their faith, is to come full circle, to replace cynicism and despair with a transfusion of childlike innocence. Only when we overcome the excuses and all the inertia of our recalcitrant hearts—only when we say our prayers on a daily basis with our children—will we find the healing we need.

STAGES OF YOUR CHILD'S SPIRITUAL LIFE

In the short introductions to the sections of prayers included in this book, we discuss many of the specific types and occasions of prayer. In this chapter, we'd like to step back and look at the larger perspective of the stages of your child's spiritual life and the prayers that are appropriate to these phases of development.

For the first two to three years of life, before we can expect a child to comprehend enough to say his own prayers, parents can wrap the child in a mantle of devotion. One analogy that supports this practice comes from the many spiritual writers today who point out the intimate relationship that can develop between the body's movements and postures and the inner disposition of the soul. Just as it is possible to learn how to pray while taking a daily walk (what's known as "prayer-walking"), so too bathing, cuddling, and singing to a child can become physical incarnations of prayer—with or without words to accompany these gestures.

In fact, we would argue (with a goodly amount of scientific evidence to back us up) that both children in the womb and infants have the capacity to know and respond to the type of love that is being communicated to them. An example of this from our own experience involves the parental blessing. We have followed the ancient practice of blessing our children each night from the day that they were born. Placing a hand on their heads, we pronounce the words of blessing and then make the sign of the cross on their foreheads. We've found that all of our kids, even if they're restless, whiny, and unwilling to go to sleep, will quiet down and receive the blessing with an expression that we can only call solemn. Our youngest child, Benedict, used to stroke Dad's outstretched forearm while he gave the blessing—a gesture of indescribable tenderness. We're convinced that our kids recognize something special, something that has the sacred character of a religious ritual, when we give them these blessings—and that they receive these blessings as gifts. Lest this sound a little too mystical, we have to report that our kids frequently return, immediately after their blessings, to their gripes and protests. (No one ever said that prayer was *magic*.)

A practice that can start when your children are very young but can continue almost indefinitely is the habit of praying *over* your children. This sort of prayer is not for everyone, since it involves the kind of spontaneous prayer that makes some people self-conscious, but it can be among the most moving and comforting of any prayers said by a parent. (Few passages in the Gospels are as poignant as those in which Christ prays out loud for those around him.) Praying over a child is just another way of wrapping her in a blanket of love and protection. Simple, heartfelt words rather than eloquence are the essence of such prayers. We provide some models for this sort of prayer in the section "Prayers for Parents, Grandparents, and All Those Who Love Children."

In attempting to sketch out the stages of a child's evolving prayer life, we have found it helpful to think in terms of four broadly defined concepts, which parallel, to a great extent, the chronological development of a child's spirituality from toddlerhood to adolescence. We don't claim scientific or clinical authority for these concepts, but they have helped us think about the interaction between prayer, spirituality, and the emotional and mental growth of children. The four concepts we have singled out are prayer as relationship, attention, participation, and transformation. It is impossible to assign specific ages for this widening progression of prayer-consciousness, for many reasons, including differing personalities and a child's age when first introduced to prayer. We can say this much: the first stage—prayer as relationship—can begin when your child is still a toddler, whereas the last stage—prayer as transformation—will probably develop fully only when your child has become a teenager. That each of these stages contains powerful, direct lessons for us grown-ups is a fact that never ceases to amaze us.

Prayer as Relationship

Small children have a natural talent for empathy. Anyone who has been around children knows that they will often look into your face and change their expression to match yours. It can be quite startling to be confronted with a little empathetic mirror whose face suddenly takes on a look of adult worry or sadness. A child's gaze can be so filled with wonder, love, and hunger for knowledge that adults, who have learned to be more guarded and emotionally defensive, can find themselves becoming uncomfortable. Our response to the gaze of a child will determine to a great extent what that child learns about the world: trust or fear, love or selfishness. Since the heart of prayer is our ability to become transparent before God, to open ourselves and our needs to the Father who loves us and seeks our well-being, then the vulnerability and openness of children is a powerful example to *us*.

Young children think in terms of relationships rather than abstractions; they look for role models rather than ideas to guide them. The same phenomenon applies to their understanding of God. As the child psychiatrist Robert Coles puts it in *The Spiritual Life of Children*, "In the lives of children, God joins company with kings, superheroes, witches, friends, brothers and sisters, parents, teachers, police, firefighters, and on and on." It takes time for a child to begin to separate God from superheroes and firefighters, but their assumption that God is a *person,* someone to whom they can talk and relate, seems to us to be just the kind of wisdom that adults tend to forget—or avoid.

Parents themselves are perhaps the single most important image for a child's understanding of God. A recent study, titled "Parent-Child Relationships and Children's Images of God," by psychologist Jane R. Dickie and a team of researchers, broke new ground in this area. In particular, they sought to discover how children perceived images of God as a "powerful, just authority and/or as a nurturing, compassionate care-giver." After studying two sample groups of children between the ages of four and eleven, Dickie and her team concluded: "Despite differences between the two samples in race, socioeconomic status, and religious affiliations, remarkably consistent findings were demonstrated. When parents were perceived as nurturing and powerful (especially when mother was perceived as powerful and father was perceived as nurturing), children perceived God as both nurturing and powerful; more like father in early childhood and more like mother or both parents in middle childhood."

Dickie's study offers some fascinating insights into the way fathers and mothers can break down sexual stereotypes and embody the virtues of authority and compassion in profound ways. But the bottom line of this study is clear—the more deeply parents are involved in their children's lives, the more balanced and profound is the image of God held by those children.

The prayers of a young child have a refreshing simplicity, even when they seem to be theologically or morally "wrong." Our children have prayed in one breath for God to bless

Mommy, Daddy, and everyone else in the family (especially our pets) and then proceed to ask God for a variety of toys and candy (using specific brand names). If we are honest, we'll recognize the same configuration of mixed motives that may attend our own prayers, and our attempts to correct our children's prayers will be correspondingly gentle. In these sweet, unselfconscious prayers, a child is learning to see God as protector and provider, the source of blessing and bounty.

A relationship involves a conversation, or at least a sense of companionship. Children often testify with remarkable confidence that Jesus has spoken to them and been present in their lives in various ways, both in times of joy and in times of sorrow.

As a child grows, there comes a recognition that a relationship with God entails an appropriate balancing of give and take; they realize that you don't ask a friend for something that is utterly self-centered or that would violate the friend's love and trust. When our daughter Helena, who was eleven at the time, received a nasty gash from a piece of broken glass, she went to the emergency room to get her arm stitched up. We asked her if she prayed in the hospital. She responded, "When I got my stitches, I said, 'Dear Father, thank you that I didn't get anything [worse] than I already have, and I hope that I can get better. Jesus, I know this is for my own good, and I know I am going to take it because if I don't, it is going to hurt even more.'" Helena did not ask for the pain to be taken away, only for the strength and courage to endure it, because Jesus wanted her wound to be healed in the right way.

Another simple but affecting story is recounted by the poet David Brendan Hopes in his memoir *A Childhood in the*

Milky Way. One night, the young Hopes was haunted by fears that Godzilla would attack his house:

That particular night, Mother and Father are going out. Mother is dressing by the pink glass lamps in her room, putting on the perfume I smell now in memory as I type. I am crying. She asks me why, and I overcome my deep inclination to say, "Oh, nothing." I tell her I am afraid.

"Of what?"

"Of monsters."

I think I expected her to make fun of me, but instead she says an amazing thing. "Why don't you pray? Ask Jesus to take the fear away."

I did, and He did. That was the beginning of a life that has been an almost uninterrupted dialogue between me and the long-suffering deity.

There have been caricatures of Christianity that treat it as nothing more than wish fulfillment or an indulgence in "magical thinking." But we have found that in prayer, a child looks to Christ not simply as a magician waving a wand but as a friend. A friend, even one with great power and resources, does not simply dole out quick and easy solutions; rather, friends help us work through our problems. Prayer, when it emerges out of a sense of a relationship with God, is grounded in moral realism—the kind of realism we noticed in Helena's account of getting her stitches. That's why we're convinced that prayer constitutes a profound engagement with reality, rather than a withdrawal from it.

Prayer as Attention

Relationships are a two-way street: in them, we both share our needs and pay attention to the needs of others. Though most young children have remarkable powers of empathy, they tend (naturally enough) to dwell on their own thoughts and emotions. But as children mature, their capacity for an imaginative grasp of the world around them increases dramatically. The world expands with their growing minds and hearts.

One of the tragedies of our times is that the natural curiosity of our children is stunted. Popular culture and high-tech gadgets provide our kids with endless distractions based on ever-increasing volumes of noise, special effects, and violence. The restless, flickering images of music videos flash across TV screens a couple of seconds at a time. Is it any wonder that attention spans are dwindling?

Though it's not likely that these trends are going to change in the foreseeable future, there are ways that parents can help nurture their children's powers of concentration. Reading aloud to children is one such method that has been championed in recent years by educators like Jim Trelease. In listening to a story, a child learns to comprehend plot, build vocabulary, evaluate character and motive, and create mental pictures of settings that are often exotic or set in the distant past.

Prayer is another means by which children (and adults) can develop their ability to attend to the world around them. The great twentieth-century poet W. H. Auden put it this way: "To pray is to pay attention to something or someone other than oneself. Whenever a man so concentrates his attention—on a landscape, a poem, a geometrical problem, an idol, or the True God—that he completely forgets his own ego and desires, he is praying. The primary task of the schoolteacher is to teach children, in a secular context, the technique of prayer."

When we pray, we develop a heightened state of awareness of the wonders of creation and our place in that creation. In prayer, children direct their gaze outward—toward God, family, and friends. When children praise or thank God, or ask for protection over loved ones, they are attending to realities that are beyond themselves.

As children grow in the life of faith, you will notice yet another facet of their attention to the world. They will become more aware of themselves—of their actions and the impact of those actions on the people around them. When a child confesses faults and pleads for help, something profoundly significant has taken place: the birth of a moral life, the first stirrings of that most precious of human capacities, the conscience. In our own family experience, we found that our kids needed a little prompting before they would confront their failings during family prayers. But soon this "examination of conscience" became a natural part of their spontaneous prayers at night.

This leads us to one of the central paradoxes of faith, as attested by nearly all of the great Christian spiritual writers: the ones who turn outward in prayer become far more vibrant individuals, more "in touch with themselves" than if they had attempted to turn their gaze inward. When your children begin to attend to the divine, they will become more deeply and fully human.

To pay attention to the world inevitably means to become more curious about it. When children begin to pray, you can expect a steady stream of mind-boggling questions. Unlike so many of us jaded grown-ups, kids are interested in wanting to know why things are the way they are. How many parents down through the ages have noticed that the questions children ask quickly become theological—even when prayer isn't a daily part of family life? Who made the world? Did God make Pepsi (a question our son Charles once asked)? What came before God? Does Jesus know what we are thinking? Why does God allow people to suffer? As a parent, you will probably find yourself feeling "theologically challenged" by all these questions. Which of us hasn't given in to the temptation to shut down our children's endless questioning? But there's no need to panic. In our experience, children will not be shocked if you admit that you're not sure of all the answers. What they *will* look for, however, is some sign that you, too, are struggling to understand, that you're willing to try to articulate some response to them. For most children, we suspect, it is enough that you are accompanying them on a journey of faith. Prayer, Bible reading, and conversation can become powerful means by which we can probe into the realm of the spirit. What else is this probing but a serious form of attention?

One of the most moving illustrations we have found of children's ability to "lose" themselves in prayer, only to vividly "find" themselves in the process, comes from Robert Coles's book, *The Spiritual Life of Children*. In a chapter titled "Representations," Coles offers descriptions of the religious pictures by children that are reproduced in his book. One of the simplest and most affecting of those pictures shows a black girl on her knees with her back to us, facing a large pink bed. Coles explains that the picture was drawn by Leola, a twelve-year-old child from a "broken-down" Georgia neighborhood. The lack of feet in Leola's picture comes not from any defect in her drawing but because she lost her legs below the knee in a car accident that killed her father.

Prayer is central to Leola's life, the time when she can hum and sing to God, to come to Him when she feels the "down and out blues":

> "I tries to be grateful that He sent me here, and if He can see that Leola is 'deceptifyin,' then He'll forgive me, because if you try to be good, and you can't get there, not all the way, then that's only making you one of His folks, and He can't expect more of you than He gave you. Oh, I talk to my legs. I tell them I'm sorry it happened to them, I'm real sorry! I tell them I won't forget them! I tell them we'll take up the slack—my arms and all I can get me to do from the waist up!"

Coles watched Leola draw her picture, and his comment on it captures the fierce attention this girl brings to her prayers:

> Then she looked at what she had drawn—the colors, her colors, her color, her body, both halved and suggestively complete in its intense and committed holding, its mix of self-affirmation and self-effacement . . . its back turned in a goodbye to itself, a hello to the Other One, who is . . . the great blank of the infinite receiving one child's picture of

devotion: a rendering of the austere aloneness of
meeting God, the transport of prayer, the call to
the world beyond worlds, the name beyond names.

One can only call Leola's faith heroic, a force that has been re-
fined and strengthened in the fires of tragedy and adversity.
Her powers of attention and her search for meaning are fierce;
in prayer, she asks questions and finds answers. Even if most
of us—children and parents alike—can't aspire to that type of
heroism, Leola's faith enables us to catch a glimpse into a
heart made wise through prayer.

Finally, it should also be remembered that prayer involves
listening as well as looking, the attempt to hear God's response to our petitions and hopes and praise. This, too, is a
form of attention, one that searches for meaning and the
mysterious ways in which God's grace touches our lives.

Prayer as Participation

Whenever the topic of the "youth generation" surfaces on the
opinion pages of newspapers and magazines, it tends to
evoke strong emotions: Are today's youth more decadent
than those of previous generations, or are they imbued with
special qualities that will help bring about social renewal?
There are merits to both sides of this debate, we suspect, but
there is one question that is perennially valid: Do young people
believe that they are vital participants in society, or are they
marked by apathy and a lack of connection with political and
cultural institutions? In a media-dominated era, are our
children becoming couch potatoes before they even reach
adolescence? The many complex problems that confront us,

both at home and abroad, won't be solved by a generation of bystanders.

Now prayer may seem like the last thing that would encourage children to participate more fully in the world around them. After all, most of us have been conditioned by decades of second-rate Freudianism to think that prayer is little more than a passing of the buck to God. To be fair to the critics, it has to be said that there is a grain of truth in this assertion—prayer *can* at times become a substitute for action. In his book *Letters to Malcolm, Chiefly on Prayer*, the great spiritual writer C. S. Lewis confessed that "I am often praying for others when I should be doing something for them."

However, we are convinced that prayer, when it is practiced in the right spirit, is a powerful means through which children can learn responsibility and a sense of engagement with the world around them. As we said in the Introduction, this is one of the central paradoxes of the spiritual life: that when we pursue heaven with true passion, we find ourselves caring more deeply for earth than we had ever imagined possible.

Now the question of whether our prayers can directly influence the course of events lands us quickly in a tangle of complicated and mysterious issues. Countless people pray every day for things that don't come to pass—from the healing of illnesses to peace on earth. It is one thing to say that our prayers are always subject to God's approval, but it is another for us to find emotional satisfaction in that idea, particularly when we suffer loss and disappointment.

Nonetheless, some intuition, buried deep in our heart, leads most of us to believe that our prayers matter, that in the divine economy, our petitions add to the balance of goodness in the universe. The Bible is full of instances when men and women bargain—often successfully—with God, obtaining clemencies and blessings. The seventeenth-century poet George Herbert described prayer as an "engine against th'Almighty," meaning by *engine* something like a catapult that hurls weapons against the fortress walls of an adversary. Prayer invites us into a passionate embrace of the world, not a withdrawal from it.

As long as children do not equate prayer with magic or instant solutions, they will continue to join the worldwide chorus of petitions to God. In the process, they begin to understand that they are not merely spectators of life but agents of change.

How is this so? As parents, we've been reminded again and again that school and family life are the twin stages on which the dramas of childhood are played out; they are the microcosms where children learn the virtues and manners that will prepare them to enter society as adults. What we've discovered during family prayer times is that our children, in sharing the hurts and anxieties they experience at home and school, develop a strong awareness of the roles they play on these stages.

When our friend Kim Alexander's eldest son started junior high school, one of the first school-related experiences of the year came about after he signed up for seventh-grade football. With one hundred kids on the team, he was plunged into chaos, what Kim calls a "*Lord of the Flies* scenario." There were plenty of swaggering bullies who would mercilessly mock anyone who seemed vulnerable. Kim's son had spent the previous summer reading Jack London novels, so he quickly recognized the dog-eat-dog environment. At one point, he got his schedule mixed up and missed the beginning of a practice. Since thirty boys had already dropped off the team—victims of two-hour practices in the heat of a Texas August—some of the boys still on the team thought his late arrival meant that he too had quit. So they locked him out of the locker room and called him a girl. He came home terribly upset. The pattern that Kim follows in such moments is to begin by speaking seriously with her son about the experience, then they make jokes about it, and finally she will pray over him.

Though Kim prays out loud *for* her son, he is still immersed in the spiritual and emotional context of prayer, which forms his whole outlook on life. Prayer gives him the courage to resist the temptations of vulgarity and brutality that surround him; it enables him to pity and forgive—and to laugh at human folly. Of course, he and his siblings have asked Kim what prayer actually accomplishes, since the class bullies are not instantly converted every time they are prayed for. Kim's reply to this question is straightforward. Suppose I walked into a classroom and asked for ten volunteers, she says. You don't have to volunteer, but the job is going to get done anyway. So why not volunteer and help complete the task? When you pray, she concludes, you are participating in the work of reconciliation and healing that God is carrying out. This may not answer every doubt in her children's minds, but it becomes a part of their reflection on their role in the small society in which they live.

There is another sense in which prayer can increase a child's feeling of active engagement with the world around him. In prayer, we have the opportunity to admit our faults, ask forgiveness, and seek reconciliation with others. Prayer clears a space in which we can put aside our egos and reflect on the consequences of our actions. We asked our daughter Magdalen about this when she was thirteen. "When I have to apologize," she said, "sometimes I don't want to become vulnerable, because that can make me just get into another fight. You don't fight in prayers, so I can open up and know that it's not going to hurt me." We've also found that during family prayers, we've admitted to the times when we failed to contribute to the daily work of the household.

When we asked the poet Scott Cairns to share his experiences with us, his response echoed that of Magdalen. Family prayers in the Cairns household, he told us, "are more like indirect conversations with each other; prayer of this sort is a useful convention for expressing love, gratitude, fear, and various other anxieties to one another in a way that does not demand direct response from spouse or child. These prayers have been, and remain, powerful moments of familial confession."

Charity begins at home, as the old saying goes. From the microcosms of home and school, a child's circle of awareness expands to the larger stages of community, nation, and "global village." The big question is whether his understanding and compassion will also widen. In our own household, we have noticed that by the time our kids reached the age of ten or eleven, they became more aware of the various crises and catastrophes reported in the news. Gradually, these events began to enter our evening prayers. Whether it be the plight of refugees fleeing from brutal civil wars or the death of a child in a fire, corresponding pleas for healing, wisdom, and consolation now rise from one home in the Pacific Northwest.

This interest in wanting to move from prayer to directly helping others can start in the smallest, most humble of ways. When our friends William and Emilie Griffin first gave one of their daughters an allowance, they were surprised when she put the entire amount into the collection basket at church. "But that's your *entire* allowance for the week," Bill Griffin remonstrated. "Well, I just gave it to God," she said. And that was that.

Prayer as Transformation

Our daughter Magdalen's understanding of prayer—that it provides for her something like a consecrated space where she can work out problems—helped us see prayer in a new light. As our children have grown, prayer has come to play a vital role in the way they process the emotional and moral challenges of daily life.

That's why prayer is the ultimate antidote to violence, one of the worst menaces plaguing our children today. If violence is an inability to work out conflicts constructively, then prayer offers a profound and life-changing alternative.

It would be misleading to say that prayer merely offers us emotional release, as if it were little more than a sanctified form of venting. Because prayer is said in the presence of God and is addressed *to* God, it is shaped and conditioned by that relationship. To be sure, there are times when we may, in moments of frustration and pain, hurl our prayers at God, as in Herbert's image of the besieger's "engine." But if we open our hearts to a loving and good Father, then we become like wayward children who have the opportunity to repair and deepen their relationship with a parent. God is the silent listener who encourages us to reveal our vulnerabilities in the context of love and trust.

There is an old cliché that compares the practice of psychological counseling and therapy to the Catholic practice of confession. Of course, an intermediary like a priest isn't a requirement for prayer. But the cliché contains a profound truth: to work through our problems, we need a sympathetic ear, an ear that allows us to explore and resolve what is inside us. To quote the poet George Herbert again, prayer invites us to offer up our "soul in paraphrase."

Most people today sense that the image of God the Father as a vengeful and judgmental listener does not represent the heart of the biblical tradition, despite the caricatures that have been drawn by both extreme secularists and fundamentalists. In the Old Testament, one of the most frequent refrains tells us that God is "slow to anger, and abounding in steadfast love." And in the New Testament, Jesus clearly prefers to let others reveal what is inside them, for better or worse. When Jesus tells those who are prepared to stone the woman taken in adultery that the person without sin must cast the first stone, he is not arguing for moral relativism. Rather, he is reminding us that God's righteousness and compassion are greater than brittle human judgments.

One reason we believe that parents and children should pray together is that they can experience in prayer this hallowed process of transformation, this laying open of hearts before the divine listener. Flannery O'Connor, whose stories and novels have been recognized as ingenious spiritual parables, was fond of the phrase "Everything that rises must converge." When we pray together, our hearts rise above petty sins and fears and converge in the heart of God.

Prayer is also a time for revelations and surprises, most of them quite pleasant. Our son Charles has spent a good deal of his youth assiduously cultivating the image of the young slacker—slouchy walk, baggy pants, reversed baseball cap, the works. And yet when it is Charles's turn to offer up some spontaneous prayers in the evening, he will speak with what we can only describe as an astonishingly supple, deeply spiritual intelligence. It is at moments like these that we realize how observant he is, both of himself and of the world around him, and how remarkable is his ability to put those observations in a prayerful context. So we are reminded, in a particularly vivid way, of how easy it is for us as parents to stereotype our own children, to make assumptions about them that fail to do them justice. To experience such moments in prayer is both chastening and exhilarating.

The spiritual writer Richard Foster has said that "to pray is to change." Once this prayerful process of transformation begins, you may find that your children are not the only ones who are changing but that you too are being changed—slowly, imperceptibly—by the invisible power of God's grace.

Praying Together as a Family

A HOW-TO GUIDE

The family is the country of the heart.

GIUSEPPE MAZZINI

Because this book is not just about the theory of prayer but a collection of prayers that you can use on a daily basis with your children, it's time to get practical. This is the hard part—moving from the desire to pray to prayer itself, or from old routines to new experiences. A thousand different things can—and do—hold us back. And even if we do begin to pray, this "habit of being" is not an easy one to maintain, at least for us grown-ups. The sheer inertia of our existing habits, our immersion in the mundane, makes it difficult for us to persevere in prayer.

GETTING STARTED: BABY STEPS

Where to begin? How can we move out of the powerful currents that flow through our lives to find the "still waters" where prayer is possible? How, in short, do we gather together as a family to break the ice with God?

The answers to these questions may vary, depending on many factors, including the ages of your children, your schedule, and your denominational and cultural backgrounds. But we think it is safe to say that there are two opportunities for family prayer that nearly everyone can make a part of the daily routine—grace before meals and evening (or morning) prayer. In fact, not only are these two forms of prayer the best places to start, but they may also become the principal prayers in your family life. A family that says grace and morning or evening prayers every day will have all the time it will ever need to grow together in grace and love.

The great advantage of these two types of prayer is that they are eminently *natural*. Prayer on such occasions is not imposed or artificial; it is something that grows out of our deepest human instincts and aspirations. Because children have not acquired adult cynicism or a jaded approach to the word, they retain a strong intuitive connection to these instincts. And because they are so dependent on others, children are less tempted than adults to believe that they can either earn or create the blessings they enjoy.

Hunger is perhaps the most vivid reminder human beings have of the fact that we are fragile creatures who depend on nourishment for our very existence. Our kids have no inhibitions about telling us when their bodies are needy or thanking us when they are satisfied. To ask a blessing before (or after) eating a meal is to acknowledge that human fragility and to celebrate the bounty of God's creation.

So it is with morning and evening prayer. When we salute the new day, we pause to take note of our rising from the symbolic death of sleep into new life and new possibilities. At the same time, we can use this quiet moment before the day's activities are upon us to commit those activities to God's hands. To make such an offering at break of day is to summon a spirit of peace that can help us—and our children—through the anxieties of the day.

As darkness falls in the evening, we may look back over the day's experiences, expressing gratitude for the good things we achieved and sorrow and regret for the bad. At night, our fears tend to emerge—from the child's fear of monsters lurking in the dark to the parent's insomniac worries about money, work, and personal relationships. To pray at close of day allows us not only to examine our hearts but also to seek comfort in God's encompassing love.

We shall delve into these ideas more fully in our introductions to these types of prayer. The point we want to make here is that grace and morning or evening prayer are the most natural places to begin family prayer. For a family that has never prayed together at all, why not begin by pausing before a meal to say a prayer of thanksgiving for the first few weeks or months? Most traditional, written table blessings are short and sweet. Even if you prefer to say a spontaneous prayer, it does not have to be long or elaborate to have a profound impact on your family. That's why such blessings before meals have come to be known simply as "saying grace." To say grace is to receive grace.

Unless your family is made up of all "morning people," the mostly likely time for daily prayer will be in the evening. When your children are quite small, the most natural time is just before sleep. Prayer, lullabies, and reading aloud are activities that simultaneously calm children down and stimulate their hearts and imaginations. Here, too, one can begin quite modestly, with a couple of short prayers and an opportunity for your child to ask God's blessing on family and friends.

Though prayer comes naturally to human beings, it is also an art. Just as a child starts by banging out random notes on the piano, only to begin formal lessons with their scales and arpeggios, so the art of prayer must begin modestly and slowly progress to the more ambitious and complex. However, the goal we seek in mastering the art of prayer is not necessarily hour-long sessions of mystical contemplation. To continue the analogy: an accomplished piano player can demonstrate just as much proficiency and ease in playing a minuet as in a full-scale concerto. So, too, the goal of learning the art of prayer should be a capacity to open our hearts to God our loving Father at any time and place, regardless of the external forms of our prayer.

What makes the analogy with learning a musical instrument so apt here (and the same could go for learning a language, sport, or nearly any other skill) is that children have an amazing capacity to absorb, adapt, and integrate knowledge. That's why we say that in family prayer, children often become the teachers.

WHEN YOU ENCOUNTER RESISTANCE

Lest we romanticize childhood too much, let's turn to a difficult issue that nearly every parent will have to confront at one point or another: What happens when a child doesn't want to pray? Given the premise of this book—that families should be praying together—the issue of a child's resistance to prayer is of paramount importance.

As a culture, we have become more willing to recognize the importance of a child's willing cooperation in behavioral change—child-rearing experts are more likely to promote incentives and encouragements rather than discipline and coercion. That tallies well with the experience of baby boomers and older generations who rebelled against religion and spirituality because it was forced on them in ways that made them feel like outsiders.

In addressing this issue, we think it is important to examine the different circumstances in which a child's reluctance to pray manifests itself. We have identified three such circumstances: (1) younger children who have not prayed before, (2) older children who have not prayed before, and (3) older children who decide to stop praying.

In our experience, children under the age of ten are unlikely to mount of full-scale rebellion against prayer. Like human beings of any age, children tend to resist anything that is new and breaks their sense of order and routine, from going off to nursery school to accepting the responsibility of doing certain chores around the house. This type of resistance may appear strong at first, but it can be surmounted after only a brief transitional phase. If you as a parent begin to pray—at meals or at night, for example—you may find that your child is observing you carefully and may even ask if she can pray. And though there will be those who disagree with us, we don't think it is wrong to insist that your child say a brief prayer or two at bedtime. Since one of the typical bedtime prayers is to ask God's blessing on family members, a child's love will quickly take over, and the initial act of parental insistence will be long forgotten.

The older a child gets, the more likely it is that his reaction to prayer will be more conscious and emotionally complicated. Let's face it: for millions of American kids, the notion of praying together as a family will hardly seem a cool thing to do. When our daughter Magdalen was fourteen, she cringed when we said grace in a restaurant. It's an understandable reaction. Though our voices are low, we make the sign of the cross and bow our heads. It was our decision—the decision to pray in public just as we prayed in private—that in Magdalen's eyes was the countercultural thing to do, as if we suffered from a particularly odd form of exhibitionism. Magdalen's instinctive embarrassment is a conventional response, which is one reason we didn't give her a hard time about it.

Despite the religiosity of the American people, there is precious little support in the public realm—and particularly in our popular culture—for something like family prayer. This climate may be changing, as the recent popularity of television programs about angels and ministers would seem to suggest, but many parents will find introducing prayer into family life to be an uphill battle.

The key to such situations is to avoid putting your children "on the spot," where they feel they have to *perform*. It is precisely at such moments that children will associate prayer with something imposed from above rather than rising up from within. The first step might be for your child to merely be present while grace or other prayers are said. You might also say the evening prayer after dinner and issue a standing invitation for anyone in the family who wishes to join you. If you are sincere about making prayer part of your life, that example will not be wasted.

The next stage might be to ask if you can pray out loud *for* your child. So long as your words celebrate and bless the child, avoiding any hint of condescension or emotional manipulation, it is hard to imagine the child objecting to this practice, once his initial self-consciousness passes. Yet another approach might be to ask the child to participate in a more formal liturgy, where his role would be merely to speak the responses. The glory of formal prayer is that it allows us to *grow into* the meaning of the words we say.

Does a child's personality have something to do with her willingness to pray? A great deal, in all likelihood. If one of your kids is extremely shy or has trouble articulating his feelings, then certain forms of prayer may prove intimidating at first. But there are so many different types of prayer that with a little experimentation, you should be able to find something that works. We have made a concerted effort to include a wide variety of prayer forms to help you find what will work in your particular situation.

There are times when a child who has been praying will want to stop. But except in situations where some extreme emotional trauma is present, this scenario usually occurs when the forms of prayer do not keep pace with the child's level of maturity. In other words, if the only model of prayer that a child experiences is that of bedtime prayer, that child's own developing mind and heart will sense a lack of spiritual stimulation and nourishment. For this reason, we suggest that you consider graduating from a few individual bedtime prayers to something more akin to a coherent ritual, in which the prayers form a brief but rounded experience.

While this may seem daunting at first, most Christian traditions have relatively simple evening prayer rituals, which sometimes go by their ancient names of Vespers or Compline. Typically, such rituals have two or three short passages from the Bible, especially the Psalms, and a short sequence of "intercessory" prayers that ask us to remember those in greatest need, such as the sick, the elderly, and the homeless.

Most of these rituals allow picking and choosing among the different prayers and readings and need not last more than five or ten minutes. What they offer older children (and their parents) is an opportunity to experience several prayers and scripture readings coming together to form a whole: an opening prayer asking for forgiveness and mercy, readings about God's lovingkindness, a series of requests for blessings for the needs of others. Each prayer sounds a particular note, but together they make a harmonious chord.

As the awareness of older children continues to expand, they will feel impelled not only to pray for the wider world but also to use prayer to understand their own personal and social development. Many of the prayers we have selected for this book may appear quite grown-up to you, but you may be surprised how quickly your kids are ready for them. Adolescence is a rough time, but if parents remain sensitive and adaptable, there is no reason why prayer cannot keep pace with your child's life.

But if your child ceases to pray or refuses to begin, all is not lost. Your love remains. Make the commitment to pray for your children every day. How our prayers affect the universe is a mystery, but you can be sure of one thing—that praying for your children will do them good, if only because it will do *you* good. Anyway, who knows how the divine economy works? In late adolescence, Suzanne began a rebellion against religion that lasted for a number of years; she went through a great deal of personal trouble and anguish before returning to her childhood faith. When Suzanne did return, her grandmother told her that she had gone to daily Mass for several years to pray for her. Her grandmother had never breathed a word of this during the entire time she had been praying. Suzanne is convinced that her grandmother's prayers did play some role in the course of her life.

GIGGLES, FIDGETS, AND PRAYERS GONE ASTRAY

Prayer has many connotations in people's minds, and one of them is of hushed cloisters and silent, candlelit temples. Well, when prayer takes place in a home with children, *hushed* is not a word that will spring to mind that often. For all their aptitude for prayer, kids are still kids, and parents will have to deal with prayers being interrupted by flying toys, wrestling matches, wandering attention spans, and the question of what to do about childish prayers that don't seem to be spiritually correct. Bedtime prayers may be a perfect way to help tuck a child into peaceful sleep, but they come at a time when your kids are the most tired (even if that is manifested in a burst of manic activity!).

One thing that we learned when our children were small was the difference between truly bad behavior and the high spirits that emerge out of the intimacy of family prayer. Some of the most raucously joyful moments we've ever had as a family have taken place just before, during, and after prayers. At such moments, our hearts are light: we seem to be more witty and satirical than usual, and irreverent in the playful way that only reverent people can be. This shouldn't be surprising. In fact, it is for us the incontrovertible proof that prayer is a form of intimate play. As parents, we tend to go easy on this sort of spirited behavior. We have also come to recognize when our kids' restlessness is caused by prayers that are too long, too late in the evening, or too elaborate for their comprehension.

At some point, however, high jinks have to give way to some form of order. Kids have to settle down, TVs and CD players have to be turned off, and some effort must be made to create a spirit of quietness. If it is necessary to discipline the children in order to achieve this, so be it. Just be careful that your own tiredness does not lead you to be so harsh with them that they associate your anger with the experience of prayer—something, alas, we have not always averted in our house. (During evening prayer, our children will occasionally parody Greg's gruff voice when he bellows out the first words of a prayer as a call to order—"GLORY BE to the . . ."— holding up a lovingly mocking mirror to Dad's behavior.)

A trickier issue arises when your child prays in an inappropriate manner—which usually means praying selfishly, asking for candy, presents, and other goodies. Of course, on the scale of sins that human beings are capable of, the wayward prayer of a tot has to rank at the very bottom. There are times when a smile of indulgence is the best response to a greedy prayer request. But there are also times when some gentle correction is justified. At such moments, we try to steer the children toward prayers of gratitude for what they already have, as well as prayers for the good of others. And as children grow older, they are more open to Christ's prayer: "Not my will but thine be done."

PLACES, POSTURES, AND SACRED SIGNS

C. S. Lewis once said that "the body ought to pray as well as the soul." Coming from a ferociously rational thinker like Lewis, this statement carries even greater weight. Words and thoughts are central to the experience of prayer, but without a bodily context, they become dry and abstract. The environment in which we pray, the positions and postures of our bodies, and the signs and symbols we use are all vital to our experience of the spiritual. We would argue that every religious tradition has its own forms of embodying prayer. Even in certain Protestant traditions, which would never countenance incense, candles, statues, and icons, there are still a few key symbols—a large, leather-bound Bible, for example, to stress the centrality of the Word of God.

Since children live in and through their bodies more intensely than adults, they respond quickly to their environments. So even though it remains true that prayers can be said anywhere and anytime, it is wise to give some attention to the environment.

If you are praying at night with small children, the obvious place to pray is in their bedrooms. This will help keep the elements of bedtime ritual—including reading aloud, brushing hair, and so on—in a single location. Our cultural memory is full of images of children kneeling by their bedside to pray, and that is certainly a hallowed tradition. When we kneel in prayer, we assuming a position of humility and vulnerability. To kneel before someone is to place yourself at the person's mercy. In our real-life experience, however, we've found that our kids find kneeling more fatiguing than we at first imagined. Kneeling is always easier to sustain when you have something to lean on, such as a bed or a chair. Some people use a small prayer bench known as a *prie-dieu* (literally, "pray God"), which consists of a padded kneeler attached to an upright section surmounted by a shelf on which a prayer book or hymnal can be placed.

But in our family, we've chosen simply to sit for our prayers. This may be influenced by the fact that we kneel a fair amount in church on Sunday, but it is also the most comfortable position, and in this instance, comfort helps us avoid the distraction of aching bones and muscles. The only posture for prayer that we don't recommend is lying down— that's an invitation for your kids to doze off prematurely!

When your children are old enough, consider praying in a common area of the house. In some traditions, such as Judaism, there is even a specific part of a room that becomes the place of prayer. Edward Hays, in *Prayers for the Domestic Church,* suggests that every family should select its "shrine-place." "This can be the table or a corner of a room or simply a spot beneath a religious icon or image." Just as we enter a church, synagogue, or mosque in order to find a sacred space conducive to prayer, so a shrine-place in the home can help us to step aside from our mundane lives for a brief time.

Prayer can also be aided by positions other than kneeling, sitting, or standing. In recent years, the ancient *orante* position—often seen in the catacomb paintings of early Christian Rome—has become popular. In this posture, the lower arms are held out at about a 45-degree angle, with elbows against the chest to avoid fatigue and the palms up. Another custom is to hold hands during prayer, as when saying grace or the Lord's Prayer. We don't recommend holding hands for long periods of time because people tend to become self-conscious about sweaty palms or trembling arms. One of the most lovely—and most neglected—of sacred gestures is the bow, which can be done at the beginning and end of prayer or at other times. Many Christians make the sign of the cross at certain points in their prayers and rituals. The "kiss of peace" (which can be an actual kiss, a hug, or a handshake) offers us a chance to express our reverence for one another. As you explore the spiritual traditions that are most nourishing for you, you will discover more about these and other gestures.

SPONTANEOUS VERSUS WRITTEN PRAYERS

A famous passage in the book of Ecclesiastes begins, "For everything there is a season, and a time for every matter under heaven: a time to be born and a time to die, a time to plant, and a time to pluck up what is planted." So it is with prayer. There is a time for using established words and forms, and there is a time to let the soul give vent to its needs and hopes in the language that comes straight from our hearts to our lips.

A book like this, with its large collection of written prayers, may seem to be weighted in the direction of formal prayer. But spontaneous prayer provides a necessary balance to written prayers: it reminds us that our words need to be intimately bound up with our feelings and intentions and that any drift between these two things will lead to spiritual inertia and emptiness. We all know instinctively what the dangers of rote language are. How many people (particularly among the baby boomers) look back with anger and perhaps a touch of cynicism to childhood experiences of rote prayer that were merely perfunctory—something that had to be done to "follow the rules" but had no heartfelt meaning. How many people drifted away from religious life altogether because of such experiences?

Children are quick to spot gaps between feeling and expression. Because they have forgiving spirits, children will be tolerant of adults who are too tired or distracted to pray properly. But if they sense an underlying lack of inner commitment on the part of the grown-ups who teach them, children will feel betrayed, and in the long run, they will shut down their spiritual sensibilities and just go through the motions required of them. The judgment of a child can be terrible indeed.

Of course, it is one thing to propose spontaneous prayer as a liberation from the tyranny of rote language and quite another thing to achieve comfort and fluency when ad-libbing prayers. Ironically, many of those who begin to pray extemporaneously find that it is far more difficult than they imagined. When this happens, disillusionment is followed by the abandonment of any type of prayer.

Children, however, are mercifully free from the kinds of self-consciousness and embarrassment that prevent adults from praying. The impromptu prayers of a child can pour out with an ease and earnestness that can fill jaded adults with awe. Kids have far fewer barriers, categories, and hierarchies than grown-ups; they haven't learned that some things are too trivial or too personal to pray for. They will beseech the Lord to look after a pet turtle and a dying grandparent in the same breath, because their love is wonderfully democratic.

But children grow and change rapidly, and they too begin to find that their extemporaneous prayers become more and more repetitive, eventually becoming just another sort of formal prayer.

So how do you avoid "spontaneous prayer fatigue"? The novelist and spiritual writer Walter Wangerin Jr. suggests that spontaneous prayers work best when there is a specific occasion to give impetus to these prayers. An example would be hearing news that a loved one is seriously ill. The prayers that arise at that moment have the freshness of newly awakened compassion.

To the extent that you can encourage your children to share what troubles them—for instance, the difficulties they encountered at school that day—their impromptu prayers will connect with their deepest needs and longings. Of course, parents have to tread lightly here because children should not be coerced into talking about matters they feel are too private to reveal.

Another technique worth trying is to read a passage from the Bible and then pause and ask the children to find a way to link that scripture to their own lives. After exploring the subject for a time, invite your children to pray about the scripture and its relevance to their lives.

Finally, don't worry too much about certain forms of repetition in your kids' prayers. After all, litanies like "God bless Mommy and Daddy, Grandma and Grandpa" are said with a love that can never be exhausted.

BY HEART: MEMORIZING PRAYERS

Now that we've just put in a plug for making spontaneous prayer a part of your family devotions, we want to move back in the other direction and promote the habit of memorizing prayers. For many years now, memorization has been rather unpopular in America—at least in our educational system. Fewer and fewer children have to memorize anything longer than a ten-line passage from Shakespeare. And yet it can be argued that the act of memorizing classic literature, scripture, and prayers might be one of the most liberating and enriching habits a human being can acquire. To memorize passages of profound wisdom and imaginative splendor is to possess great treasure indeed. An older term for memorization is to learn something *by heart*. Notice that the phrase isn't to learn *by head*—because this knowledge helps shape our emotions and judgment. It is much more than mere information.

And lo and behold, here is yet another faculty that children have in abundance. The flexible mind of a child can memorize vast amounts of material—amounts that adults would have to strain to remember. When it comes to prayer, memorization becomes a tremendous asset. As important as spontaneous prayer is, there are times when we don't have the mental or spiritual energy to make up our own words. And there are times when words that are far greater and more poetic than ours will stand us in good stead. What could be more comforting when one is assailed by fear or danger or the tragic reality of illness and death than to have the Twenty-Third Psalm on one's lips?

Our children know about twenty prayers by heart, including the Lord's Prayer and the Twenty-Third Psalm. Often our evening prayer consists of a medley of prayers we've memorized, topped off at the end by the spontaneous requests and thanks that occur to us at that moment. We can do this anywhere, anytime, without needing books or props of any kind.

We've even taught our children several prayers in Latin. That may strike you as bizarre, pretentious, or just plain misguided. How can a living prayer be said in a dead language? And yet when we say the Lord's Prayer in Latin, we see it through a different lens and connect in some mysterious way with a rich part of our cultural legacy. It's also an opportunity to think about the Latin roots of words we use every day.

We're not advocating the revival of Latin, but we do believe that committing prayers to memory is something that will nourish your family's spirituality. The length and complexity of the prayers is not the issue. The key is to let them take up residence in your heart.

FIGHTING BOREDOM: REPETITION AND VARIETY

Whatever we do on a daily basis can, and always does, become stale and routine. That's the human condition: we cannot sustain the kind of heightened awareness and emotional vitality that we ought to. The Zen masters teach that we need to practice habits of mind and body to achieve a state of "mindfulness," so that we do not sleepwalk through our lives. The spiritual life is always about strengthening our *conscious* love, gratitude, and sensitivity to the needs of others.

Many people fear that if they begin praying—on their own or with their children—they will not be able to avoid boredom.

Yet no one would dream of *not* saying "I love you" to one's spouse every day just because tiredness or distraction diminished the emotional intensity behind the phrase. Our hearts may not always be in sync with what is on our lips, but we *must* speak what is good and true and beautiful, if only to remind ourselves of the need to live up to those things as often as we can.

So here's the unvarnished truth: praying with your children *will* occasionally be perfunctory. You may also experience what spiritual writers call "dryness," the feeling that God is absent. At moments like this, the worst thing to do is to stop praying. As we have stressed, prayer is an art and therefore depends on discipline. The great thing about discipline is that it enables us to span the gaps—to trek through dry spells to the oases that we will eventually discover. It is important that we exercise patience in our spiritual journeys, that we trust that over time we will experience real progress— a lessening of boredom and a greater serenity during periods of dryness. What a gift to a child if you are able to impart this lesson early in life.

That said, we do practice a number of antiboredom tactics in our household. We use three different graces, for example. Our evening prayers also take different forms. The more formal evening prayer we say now with our three older kids has built-in variety: the prayer book has different psalms, scripture readings, and prayers each day. But we also practice our "prayer medley," and we have the occasional evening when *all* our prayers are spontaneous. Occasionally, we throw in a little Latin to spice things up. Discover your own seasoning and add to taste.

PRAYER AND READING ALOUD: FROM SCRIPTURE TO ADVENTURE STORIES

Praying and reading aloud have gone together so naturally, and have been so profoundly enriching for us and our children, that we can no longer imagine the two things separately. They are like the Fourth of July and fireworks, Gilbert and Sullivan, hot pastrami and rye. Though the two activities are distinct, they share many wonderful resonances. Literature and prayer both use heightened forms of language to lift us out of our mundane existence and put us into a more contemplative frame of mind. Both require us to listen, and to speak, with care. They also call on us to use our imaginations actively, in a way that is simultaneously demanding and pleasurable.

Most of us have heard about the studies that show the link between reading aloud and a child's performance in school. But we think the analysis should be taken a step further. In an era that is dominated by passive media like television and interactive media that are still better for pragmatic information than they are for imagination, we believe that prayer and reading aloud provide a needed balance for your child's development—the spiritual and mental "food groups" that make a proper diet for the soul.

In her book *Homeward Voyage,* Emilie Griffin captures the essence of the way prayer and reading aloud can be mutually reinforcing. Writing of the role her grandmother and aunt played in her New Orleans childhood, Griffin recalls:

They were charmers, spellbinders, storytellers.
I loved to hear them talk, and their talk was always

intermingled with a kind of prayer. They were the ones who taught me to pray, intertwining prayer and storytelling at bedtime, in a way so enjoyable that I hardly ever wanted it to end. I remember how much both [of them] loved nursery rhymes and loved to read them with me. [My aunt] taught me how verses galumphed; she made it exciting to read. They taught me prayer by example. Each morning they devoted time to Bible reading; at any time in their conversation, it seemed, a Bible saying could slip naturally in.

Griffin reminds us that faith and imagination are two human faculties that children love to exercise. Through metaphor, symbol, and rhythm, they allow us to penetrate the surfaces of things and grasp meaning.

In our house, we always pray first and then read aloud. That guarantees that if anyone gets sleepy, we can call it a night and prayer won't lose out. Since prayer can seem a little like work at times, this habit also allows the reading aloud to feel like the special treat.

INTERFAITH AND INTERDENOMINATIONAL FAMILIES: FINDING UNITY AMID DIFFERENCES

One of the most challenging situations facing anyone who wants to begin or deepen family prayer is when parents come from different faith traditions (including unbelief). In recent decades, there has been a concerted effort in our culture to celebrate the common elements in different religious traditions—an effort that has brought about greater under-standing and important messages about tolerance. And in the Christian communion, the work of ecumenism is always going on.

The truth remains that religious differences are real and should not always be passed over lightly. Some people choose to construct their own set of beliefs, but others prefer the con-crete experiences of specific religious communions, experiences that are rooted in history, scripture, culture, and theology.

How can parents with divergent perspectives create an en-vironment in which family prayer can take place?

The answers to this question are various, and few of them are easy. Some couples make an agreement that their children will be raised in either the father's or the mother's faith tradition. But there are times when agreements like this founder—as when one of the parents experiences a change of heart—and tensions inevitably follow. Some parents attempt to expose their children to both traditions, even to the extent of going to two different weekly worship services. Others find that they simply have to eliminate any practice of prayer or devotion in the home in order to avoid creating an emotional minefield.

The choice to live out some type of "both-and" approach will prove to be the most challenging on a day-to-day basis. To try to understand the challenge better, we asked our friend Leah Buturain to share her experience with us. Leah is Catholic, and her husband, Ed, is Jewish. Leah spoke frankly about the tensions and tribulations of an interfaith house-hold, but she stressed that even in the muddle of daily life, "prayer is all the more essential as a way to seek strength and unity beyond and in the midst of differences."

Like many parents in interfaith marriages, Leah works very hard to expose her children to the riches of both traditions. She takes the kids to Mass on Sunday, but they also frequently celebrate Shabbat and the Passover Seder. Also, as in many Jewish-Christian families, there is a special emphasis on the shared Jewish heritage. The most frequent prayers in the Buturain home are said in Hebrew: the *Sh'ma* ("Hear, O Israel, the Lord our God, the Lord is One") and a grace ("Blessed art thou, O Lord our God, ruler of the universe, who bringest forth this bread from the earth").

Rather than dissecting the two traditions into doctrines, Leah tries to convey to her children the cultural richness that wells up from both Judaism and Christianity. As she wrote to us:

> All the arts enrich our family's prayer life: when celebrating Shabbat or a Jewish holiday, I put on CDs of klezmer music . . . [and] my husband and I play the violin and piano and sing *Hava Nagila* while the children dance. During Advent, I play more Gregorian chants and Palestrina, the Brahms Requiem, and other classical selections, and at Christmas, we play a variety of classical, R&B, and folk music. Ed plays Yiddish and Hebrew folk songs, such as "Rozhinkes mit Mandelen" ("Raisins and Almonds"), and other beautiful songs.

Still, for all the beauty of these moments, the Buturains acknowledge that conflicts continue to arise, symbolized in a bittersweet way by their son Samuel, who says to people, "I am Jewish and I am Christian," illustrating this by drawing an imaginary vertical line down the center of his body.

Ed wrote to us: "I believe that the prayer in interfaith couples should be one that welds together both faiths but offends neither. I love my four-year-old daughter's simple prayer: 'Thank you God for our food, thank you for everything.'" This may sound like nothing more than a "lowest common denominator" approach, but there is much to recommend Ed's words. Prayer and spirituality are such fertile things that even stripped down to the bare essentials, they can grow in your children's hearts.

We are grateful to Ed and Leah for being so honest about the ongoing struggles they face. Leah has taken comfort in the image of the pilgrim in Dante's great poem, *The Divine Comedy:*

> I am keenly aware of where I wish we would be,
> able to kneel down together and pray as a unified
> family. Yet, as Dante wrote, part of loving is learning
> to prefer the given. Instead of comparing ourselves
> to other families, I read aloud Psalm 139 and
> contemplate the unique identities we have been
> given. My hope is that all of our family prayers and
> rituals will participate in a procession much larger
> than ourselves, with a community of believers who
> have preceded us and who will follow us as well.

May we all have the grace to find our place in that procession.

MOVING OUTWARD: FROM THE FAMILY TO THE LARGER COMMUNITY

As a child's horizons expand, so will her prayers, moving outward from the circle of the family to the larger world. At some point in this process, you may find that you or your children develop a desire to act on this expanding awareness. One impulse will be to move from merely praying for the less fortunate to actively serving them. The other impulse will be to participate in a larger community of prayer.

We can think of few more important lessons to teach a child than the need to link our words to deeds—to practice what we pray. Prayer is a powerful means through which we develop the motivation to "walk the walk" as well as "talk the talk." One of the easiest ways to help your children make this connection is to set aside a little money each week, even if it is little more than pocket change, for the poor or for a particular cause. In many Christian churches, the season of Lent offers families the opportunity to practice self-denial by setting aside money for the poor. Teenagers are old enough to do volunteer work for soup kitchens and other relief organizations. Prayer may strengthen our desire to serve, but service will inflame and renew our prayers. The final sections of prayers in this book are specially geared to prayers for justice and peace.

The desire to pray with a larger community of believers may prove to be a little more controversial or more complicated than public service. After all, many people find themselves either temporarily or permanently without a church home. Some have developed withering critiques of the sins of the "institutional church." And so there are families who opt to do their own spiritual thing, independent of any institution.

On the other hand, we have heard an increasing number of stories about baby boomers having second thoughts about leaving the institutional church and also about members of Generations X, Y, and beyond who leave their parents at home on the Sabbath to seek out and join a variety of worshiping communities. This brings to mind something else that Leah Buturain shared with us. She believes that even if parents have had bad memories of formal worship in their own childhood, "giving the children an opportunity to experience the rituals and services in churches and synagogues, perhaps with friends or other family members, can give us the chance to see these things with fresh eyes. . . . As much as possible," Leah continues, "we try not to project our adult issues onto our children. I admire parents who, in Coleridge's words about reading fiction, 'willingly suspend their disbelief' regarding rituals and religious observances to give their children the opportunity to feel for themselves, without any tincture of the parent's prejudice." So if one or more family members feel the need to become involved in the larger community, our hope is that they would be encouraged in that quest. For those who may be apprehensive about full membership in a church or synagogue, there are many "parachurch" organizations, from youth groups to Bible study classes, that provide something a little less institutional and yet still embrace a larger concept of spiritual community.

If you cannot pray in the synagogue,
pray in your field. If you cannot
pray in your field, pray in your house.
If you cannot pray in your house,
pray on your bed. If you cannot pray
on your bed, meditate in your heart.

MIDRASH ON PSALM 4:9

THE PRAYERS

~

Morning Prayers

Mornings seem to be the special province of young children. As long as they don't stay up too late, children have the ability to wake up with an ease and freshness that is truly astonishing. Unfortunately (but understandably), most grown-ups find it a little hard to appreciate this fact at six or seven in the morning, when young feet begin scampering down stairs or the sides of the crib begin to rattle and shake and small, insistent voices cry out for liberation.

Perhaps here, as in so many other aspects of our lives, children can remind us of something that we adults—with all our burdens, responsibilities, and anxieties—have lost sight of: that mornings should be greeted with wonder and gratitude.

If each morning is a new beginning, then it is also an opportunity to set the tone for the day, to put things into a certain perspective. Even the briefest of prayers in the morning can help lift us out of the concerns and worries that all too quickly begin to preoccupy our thoughts and emotions. And for all their innocence, children too can become weighed down by the challenges of the coming day, whether it be a big test, a crucial sports event, or just the difficulty of finding friends and navigating the waters of their social life.

What kinds of prayer are appropriate for you and your children in the mornings? A lot depends on who gets up when. As members of the household straggle down at different times and in different conditions, the notion of the entire family joining together in prayer may be a little idealistic. Nevertheless, there may be a moment—between scarfing down a bowl of cereal and running for the bus—when a common prayer might be offered.

In our family, where both Mom and Dad are emphatically "night people," it isn't practical to have family prayers in the morning. So we have encouraged our children to develop their own short, private devotions. In some traditions, a physical gesture, such as the sign of the cross, is the first and simplest act of prayer.

When it comes to using words, a single verse of scripture or a classic prayer set to a simple rhyming scheme can also be sufficient. One of our favorite morning prayers is "This is the day the Lord has made; we will rejoice and be glad in it" (Psalm 118:24).

Praise and thanksgiving are natural sorts of prayers to offer in the morning, but so are requests for guidance and wisdom in facing the particular challenges that lie ahead. You may find that your child is able to express concerns in prayer that he or she is not as ready to share in normal conversation.

Even when morning prayers begin to fade from the mind, they can still serve, at a deep psychic and emotional level, to insulate your child from fears and temptations and to inspire hope and courage.

～

Guardian angel, protect me today,
Watch over me while I work and play.
Let me be kind and loving and good,
Help me do the things I should.
    —Anonymous

Now, before I run to play,
Let me not forget to pray
To God Who kept me through the night
And waked me with the morning light.
Help me, Lord, to love Thee more
Than I ever loved before,
In my work and in my play,
Be Thou with me through the day. Amen.
    —Anonymous

For this new morning and its light,
For rest and shelter of the night,
For health and food, for love and friends,
For every gift His goodness sends
We thank you, gracious Lord. Amen.
    —Anonymous

Dear Lord, I offer you this day
All I shall think or do or say.
    —Anonymous

Day by day, dear Lord of you
Three things I pray:
To see you more clearly,
To love you more dearly,
To follow you more nearly,
Day by day.
    —Saint Richard of Chichester

Teach me, my God and King,
In all things thee to see,
That what I do in anything,
To do it as for thee.
    —George Herbert

This is the day that the Lord has made;
Let us rejoice and be glad in it.
    —Psalm 118:24

Lord of all hopefulness, Lord of all joy,
Whose trust, ever childlike, no cares could destroy.
Be there at our waking, and give us, we pray,
Your bliss in our hearts, Lord, at the break of the day.
    —Traditional Irish hymn

Let the words of my mouth, and the meditation
of my heart, be acceptable in Thy sight,
O Lord, my strength, and my redeemer.

—Psalm 19:14

O Lord, Our Heavenly Father, Almighty and
Everlasting God, who has safely brought us to
the beginning of this day; defend us in the same
with Thy mighty power; and grant that this day
we fall into no sin, neither run into any kind of
danger; but that all our doings may be ordered
by Thy governance, to do always what is righteous
in Thy sight; through Jesus Christ our Lord. Amen.

    —Book of Common Prayer

Shew me thy ways, O Lord;
teach me thy paths.
Lead me in truth, and teach me:
For thou art the God of my salvation;
On thee do I wait all the day.

    —Psalm 25:4–5

O Lord our God, grant us grace to desire you
with our whole heart, that, so desiring, we may
find you; and so finding you, we may love
you; and so loving you, may rejoice in you
for ever; through Jesus Christ our Lord. Amen.

    —Saint Anselm

May my mouth praise the love of God this morning.
O God, may I do your will this day.
May my ears hear the words of God and obey them.
O God, may I do your will this day.
May my feet follow the footsteps of God this day.
O God, may I do your will this day.

I bind unto myself today
The power of God to hold and lead,
His eye to watch, his might to stay,
His ear to hearken to my need,
The wisdom of my God to teach,
His hand to guide, his shield to ward;
The word of God to give me speech,
His heavenly host to be my guard.
>   —From the prayer known as
>   "The Breastplate of Saint Patrick"

God, who hast folded back the mantle of the night
to clothe us in the golden glory of the day,
chase from our hearts all gloomy thoughts
and make us glad with the brightness of hope.
>   —Ancient Collect

Lord Jesus Christ, you are the sun that always rises,
but never sets. You are the source of all life, creating
and sustaining every living thing. You are the source
of all food, material and spiritual, nourishing us in
both body and soul. You are the light that dispels the
clouds of error and doubt, and goes before me every
hour of the day, guiding my thoughts and my actions.
May I walk in your light, be nourished by your food, be
sustained by your mercy, and be warmed by your love.
>   —Desiderius Erasmus

Evening Prayers

What is it about evening that makes it such an appropriate time for prayer? Perhaps the most obvious answer is that the preoccupations and distractions of the day are over and that darkness brings with it a quieter, more introspective mood. But for a child, there is more to it than that. Young children often find going to sleep a difficult and even scary experience. After all, it is the time when witches fly and "things go bump in the night." Bedtime prayers serve as a sort of bridge between the day and the unconsciousness of sleep—a moment to gather together thoughts of love and trust.

A parent's presence at bedtime prayers is essential, even if the parent doesn't pray with the child. A mother or father becomes a witness to the child's prayer, another ear besides

God's. This point is worth emphasizing: the parent's presence at bedtime prayers is not just window dressing. A number of scholarly studies have demonstrated that a child's image of God is closely related to the character and personality of his parents. That's a daunting—perhaps a paralyzing—thought for most of us. Most parents know that they are fallible and far from Christlike (though we don't often admit it to our kids!). But in the long run, there is something deeply encouraging about a child's linking of God and parents. To be given the task of communicating God's unconditional love to our children is an awesome responsibility, but it is also a privilege. We may be "broken vessels," to use biblical language, but despite the leaks, we can still pass along a taste of divine grace.

Needless to say, the rituals of bedtime are profoundly important to children. As soon as prayers are over, the child is tucked into bed, flush with the feelings of warmth and comfort generated by the intimate sharing that prayer brings about. It is at moments like this that we can see the "sacramental" dimension of faith, the necessary link between the body and the spirit. We all experience love through the senses, but children are the ultimate sensualists. The smell of our father's aftershave, the sound of our mother crooning a lullaby, and above all the touch of caressing hands—these are the sacraments of love, the very foundations of our emotional well-being.

After evening prayers are over, we suggest one more action before kissing your kids goodnight. A wonderful practice that is now all but forgotten is the parental blessing (see page 70). Modern parents may be embarrassed at the idea of putting their hand on a child's head and pronouncing a blessing, as if they were some sort of priest or minister. But nothing can match the blessing of a parent for bringing a child a feeling of total security and love. We're confident that any feelings of embarrassment you may feel on giving your child a blessing will quickly disappear as you look into your child's eyes.

We have blessed our children since they were infants. Over the years, there have been evenings when we've put the kids to bed and collapsed onto the sofa, ready to watch a video or dive into a mystery novel, when we've heard the patter of little feet and seen a sleepy face appear at the door of the living room. "You forgot to bless me, Dadda," a child has said, somewhat indignantly, as if her father were the world's worst-ever absent-minded professor. When Greg is out of town on business trips, our daughter Helena asks him to bless her over the phone.

Traditionally, evening prayer is the time when one makes an examination of conscience, going over one's actions during the day, confessing sins and failings, and asking for forgiveness and grace to improve. Far from its being a strictly negative activity or "downer," a child can find in this examination of conscience an opportunity to relieve a weight of guilt and hurt. As we've mentioned, a child can often find the sharing of painful emotions easier and more "objective" in the context of prayer than in a direct, face-to-face confrontation with parents.

When children are older, the best time for saying evening prayer as a family is usually just before or just after dinner. By linking these prayers to the meal, there is less likelihood that they will be missed. Of course, many families today don't even eat dinner together, so the idea of family prayers may strike some as hopelessly idealistic. But then we set up ideals so that we can at least strive to reach for them.

⌇

God watches over us all the day,
At home, at school, and at our play,
And when the sun has left the skies,
He watches with a million eyes.
   —Gabriel Setoun

Lord, keep us safe this night.
Secure from all our fears.
May angels guard us while we sleep,
Till morning light appears.
   —Anonymous

Father, unto thee I pray,
Thou hast guarded me all day;
Safe I am while in thy sight,
Safely let me sleep tonight.
Bless my friends, the whole world bless;
Help me to learn helpfulness;
Keep me ever in thy sight;
So to all I say good night.
   —Henry Johnstone

SOME PEOPLE have expressed reservations about the following prayer, "Now I lay me down to sleep," particularly the sentence "And if I die before I wake, I pray the Lord my soul to take." It is true that this sentence might cause some confusion and anxiety in the mind of a small child, but we believe that older children can handle it. After all, human life is a fragile thing, and any Christian spirituality that does not take our mortality into account is little more than escapism. In our family, our older children have had to come to terms with the deaths of several schoolmates, and as parents, we feel that this prayer is all the more comforting because it takes all of reality into account and enfolds it in God's love.

Now I lay me down to sleep,
I pray the Lord my soul to keep.
Four corners to my bed,
Four angels there aspread:
Two to foot and two to head,
And four to carry me when I'm dead.
If any danger come to me,
Sweet Jesus Christ deliver me.
And if I die before I wake,
I pray the Lord my soul to take.
Angel sent by God to guide me,
Be my light and walk beside me;
Be my guardian and protect me;
On the paths of life direct me.
   —Anonymous

Angel of God, my guardian dear,
to whom God's love commits me here;
Watch over me throughout the night,
keep me safe within your sight.
   —Traditional Christian prayer

Protect us, Lord, as we stay awake; watch over us as we sleep, that awake we may keep watch with Christ, and asleep, rest in his peace.

—Traditional Christian prayer

God be in my head, and in my understanding;
God be in my eyes, and in my looking;
God be in my mouth, and in my speaking;
God be in my heart, and in my thinking;
God be at my end, and in my departing.

—*Sarum Primer,* fifteenth century

Now the day is over,
Night is drawing nigh,
Shadows of the evening
Steal across the sky;
Jesus, give the weary
Calm and sweet repose;
With thy tenderest blessing
May our eyelids close.
Grant to little children
Visions bright of thee;
Guard the sailors tossing
On the deep blue sea.
Comfort every sufferer
Watching late in pain;
Those who plan some evil
From their sins restrain.
Through the long night watches,
May thine angels spread

Their white wings above me,
Watching round my bed.
When the morning wakens,
Then may I arise
Pure and fresh and sinless
In thy holy eyes.
      —Sabine Baring-Gould

Jesus, Tender Shepherd, hear me;
Bless thy little lamb tonight;
Through the darkness be thou near me,
Keep me safe till morning light.
All this day thy hand has led me,
And I thank thee for thy care;
Thou hast warmed me, clothed and fed me;
Listen to my evening prayer!
Let my sins be all forgiven;
Bless the friends I love so well:
Take us all at last to heaven,
Happy there with thee to dwell.
      —Mary Duncan

Good night! Good night!
Far flies the light;
But still God's love
Shall flame above,
Making all bright.
Good night! Good night!
      —Victor Hugo

Lord, now you let your servant go in peace;
your word has been fulfilled:
my own eyes have seen the salvation
which you have prepared in the sight of every people:
a light to reveal you to the nations;
and the glory of your people Israel.

—Luke 2:29-32, known historically as the *Nunc Dimittis*

The Lord is my shepherd: I shall not want.
He maketh me to lie down in green pastures:
he leadeth me beside the still waters.
He restoreth my soul:
he leadeth me in the paths of righteousness for his
    name's sake.
Yea, though I walk through the valley of the shadow
    of death,
I will fear no evil: for thou art with me:
thy rod and thy staff they comfort me.
Thou preparest a table before me in the presence of
    mine enemies:
thou anointest my head with oil:
my cup runneth over.
Surely goodness and mercy shall follow me all the
    days of my life:
and I shall dwell in the house of the Lord forever.

—Psalm 23

Visit this house,
we beg you, Lord,
and banish from it
the deadly power of the evil one.

May your holy angels dwell here
to keep us in peace,
and may your blessing be always upon us.
We ask this through Christ our Lord. Amen.
   —Ancient Christian prayer

Watch thou, dear Lord, with those who wake, or watch,
or weep tonight, and give Thine angels charge over those
who sleep. Tend Thy sick ones, O Lord Christ. Rest thy
weary ones. Bless thy dying ones. Soothe thy suffering
ones. Pity thine afflicted ones. Shield thy joyous ones.
And all, for thy love's sake.
   —Saint Augustine

Be thou my vision, Lord of my heart;
Naught be all else to me, save that thou art;
Thou my best thought, by day or night,
Waking or sleeping, thy presence my light.
   —Eighth-century Irish hymn, translated
      by Mary Byrne and Eleanor Hall

O Lord, grant that this night
we may sleep in peace.
And that in the morning
our awakening may also be in peace.
May our daytime
be cloaked in your peace.
Protect us and inspire us
to think and act only out of love.
Keep far from us all evil;
may our paths be free from all obstacles

from when we go out
until the time we return home.
    —From the Babylonian Talmud

IN OUR HOME, the final prayer of the evening is a parental blessing. To bless your child, place one or both of your hands on your child's head and speak the blessing. Some Christians then trace the sign of the cross on the child's forehead. In our house, we finish off with a hug and a kiss.

> Lord Jesus Christ,
> Protect, watch over, and bless this child [or *substitute*
>   *the child's name*]
> With a lively faith,
> A fervent charity,
> And a courageous hope of reaching your kingdom.
>   —Anonymous

> Christ is shepherd over you,
> Enfolding you on every side.
> Christ will not forsake you, hand or foot,
> Nor let evil come near you.
>   —Anonymous

Holy Days

E very December, columnists write editorials lamenting the commercialization of the holiday season. These columns may well be the only items printed on the op-ed page during the course of the year that absolutely no one disagrees with. We read these columns, shake our heads, sigh, and think of similar problems with Valentine's Day, Saint Patrick's Day, and Halloween.

Living as we do in a materialistic culture obsessed with consumption, our pursuit of holiday happiness seems to leave everyone dissatisfied. Even Advent services and performances of the *Nutcracker* can sometimes fail to lift the flagging emotions of both parents and their kids. For most of us, the hope is that we can somehow catch glimpses of the holiday spirit in the midst of all the holiday stress.

When do those fleeting moments of holiday joy seem to burst suddenly into our hearts? Isn't it in the quieter moments, when the family draws together and shares laughter, conversation, and the simple pleasures of good food and drink, that we experience that elusive happiness?

We think that prayer offers a similar oasis of quietness and intimacy. Prayer enables us to stop our relentless activity and enter a period of time that is sacred, time that is devoted—set aside—for a high and holy celebration.

What we've lost, in this secular, technocratic society of ours, is a sense of *festivity*. The word is derived from *feast*, and another variation, of course, is *festival*. A feast day, in our spiritual tradition, is not simply a day for gorging on food (although good food, and plenty of it, is an indispensable part of it!). Rather, on a feast day, we set aside work and school to participate in a sacred ritual. Such rituals recount stories that give meaning to our lives—stories like that of the Christ child, born in obscurity and poverty, whose life and teaching about the good news of God's unconditional love would turn the world upside down.

Prayer can help us restore the spirit of festivity to family life. Children have a natural love for pomp and ceremony: the images, words, songs, and pageants form a sort of "sacred game" that many kids find fascinating. It's also amazing how much knowledge and history a child can absorb, with relatively little pain or resistance, when caught up in the spirit of a festive occasion. And as we've stressed, prayer and laughter are close cousins. When we lift up our hearts, we are lifted out of ourselves and our daily anxieties. Laughter, like prayer, wells up when we are able to step outside the grind and see things in a new perspective. That's a liberating feeling.

The prayers and rituals that are associated with most of our spiritually rooted holidays are rich and rewarding, from Advent wreaths and calendars to "hot cross buns" and lamb-shaped cakes during Lent and Easter.

If singing is "praying twice," as the old saying has it, then the holidays are a veritable feast of hymns and carols. We can only offer a small selection of the prayers that are tradition-ally said during these holidays; you will certainly find more for yourselves!

To supplement your family's prayers during the holidays, there are also many wonderful stories that encapsulate the spiritual meaning of festivals like Christmas and Hanukkah—stories that deserve to be read out loud. For younger children, there are many delightful holiday tales, such as Henry van Dyke's *Story of the Other Wise Man*. Older children might find themselves caught up in Dickens's *Christmas Carol* or Dylan Thomas's haunting *Child's Christmas in Wales*. If you don't feel up to dramatic readings of books like these, there are memorable versions on tape, performed by professional actors. Then there are plays and musical performances, such as Handel's *Messiah*. Here in Seattle, the dramatic version of C. S. Lewis's classic children's story, *The Lion, the Witch, and the Wardrobe*, seems to be a new Christmas tradition at a local children's theater.

Catholics, Orthodox, and some other denominations also observe certain feasts and memorials on saints' days. Learning to live according to the rhythms of the "church year" can be a rewarding experience for many families and can be explored more fully by learning more about a specific de-nomination or tradition.

ADVENT AND CHRISTMAS

THERE'S NO BETTER TIME OF YEAR to reconnect "holiday magic" to its ultimate sources in spirituality than the Advent and Christmas season. Ironically, the season of Advent, which is the four weeks leading up to Christmas and boasts many of the most charming and memorable customs in the history of Christianity, is also one of the most neglected seasons in the church year. Like Lent, Advent traditionally involves some form of self-denial, the better to welcome the feast of the birth of Christ. But Advent is also the time for lighting candles, blessing candy canes, opening special calendars, and a host of other customs from around the world.

Children can't wait for Christmas, yet much of their joy comes from the anticipation of presents and good things to eat. Advent prayers can link both the sacred and profane forms of expectations, reminding us that all gifts should evoke gratitude and a spirit of sharing with others.

Christmas offers us a wonderful chance to celebrate childhood itself. The essence of Christmas is the mystery of God's willingness to take on flesh, to share our human life. The Christ child is not born into power or wealth but comes into the world in the humblest of circumstances, confounding the assumptions of worldly rulers and scholars. Christmas prayers encourage us all to become a little more childlike. This is the mystery of the Incarnation.

Saint Nicholas's Day Blessing of Candy Canes (December 6)

Good Saint Nicholas, we honor you
on this your holy feast day.
We rejoice that you are the patron saint
and the holy symbol of joy
for many peoples of many lands.
Come, great-hearted saint,
and be our patron and companion
as we, once again, prepare our homes and hearts
for the great feast of Christmas,
the birth of the Eternal Blessing, Jesus Christ.
May these sweets, these candy canes,
be a sign of Advent joy for us.
May these candy canes,
shaped just like your Bishop's staff,
be for us a sign of your benevolent care.
We rejoice that you are the holy bringer of gifts
and that so many have been delighted
through your great generosity.
Help us to be as generous of heart.
Wherever these candy canes are hung,
on tree or wall or door,
may they carry with them
the bright blessing of God.
May all who shall taste them
experience the joy of God
upon their tongues and in their hearts.
We ask God, now, to bless

these your brightly striped sweets
in the name of the Father,
and of the Son,
and of the Holy Spirit. Amen.
　　—Edward Hays

Christmas Prayers

What can I give Him,
Poor as I am?
If I were a shepherd,
I would give Him a lamb;
If I were a wise man,
I would do my part;
But what can I give Him?
Give Him my heart.
　　—Christina Rossetti

A babe lies in the cradle,
A little babe so dear,
With noble light he shineth
As shines a mirror clear,
This little babe so dear.
The babe within the cradle
Is Jesus Christ our Lord;
To us all peace and amity
At this good time afford,
Thou Jesus Christ our Lord!
O Jesus, babe beloved!
O Jesus, babe divine!

How mighty is thy wondrous love!
Fill thou this heart of mine
With that great love of thine! Amen.
　　—Traditional German carol

Make me pure, Lord: Thou art holy;
Make me meek, Lord: Thou wert lowly;
Now beginning, and alway:
Now begin, on Christmas Day.
　　—Gerard Manley Hopkins

God, who became as we are,
may we become as you are.
　　—After William Blake

Glory be to God in the highest,
and on earth peace,
good will toward men.
　　—Luke 2:14

Holy Child of Bethlehem,
whose parents found no room in the inn;
we pray for all who are homeless.
Holy Child of Bethlehem,
born in a stable;
we pray for all who are living in poverty.
Holy Child of Bethlehem,
rejected stranger;
we pray for all who are lost, alone,
all who cry for loved ones.

Holy Child of Bethlehem,
whom Herod sought to kill;
we pray for all in danger,
all who are persecuted.
Holy Child of Bethlehem,
a refugee in Egypt;
we pray for all who are far from home.
Holy Child of Bethlehem,
in you the Eternal was pleased to dwell;
help us, we pray, to see the divine image
in people everywhere.
In your name we offer this prayer.
    —David Blanchflower

We pray you, Lord, to purify our hearts
that they may be worthy to become your dwelling-place.
Let us never fail to find room for you,
but come and abide in us,
that we also may abide in you,
for at this time you were born into the world for us,
and live and reign, King of kings and Lord of lords,
now and forever.
    —William Temple

LENT AND EASTER

LENT IS A SEASON that often gets a bad rap, as if it were about nothing more than denying ourselves certain pleasures. "What are you giving up for Lent?" is the question everyone wants to ask in our house. It's been said that to balance the seemingly negative idea of giving something up, it is worth considering taking something on, such as some form of service or prayer. (Whenever Greg says he's going to do that, our kids snicker, as if he's just taking the easy way out!)

Whether you do without something or take on some good work, the point is that Lent is a time of reflection and reevaluation. In the forty days between Ash Wednesday, which reminds us of our mortality, and Easter, when we celebrate the resurrection of Christ and his triumph over death, Lent offers us an opportunity to draw closer to God, to clear away some of the debris in our hearts that gets in the way of a more intimate relationship with the Creator.

There are some who may consider Lent too grim to provide much that is edifying for children, but we beg to differ. Children have an innate need to understand sin, death, and suffering; we do them a disservice if we make spirituality about nothing more than emotional uplift. They also respond to the idea that sacrifice is a form of gratitude, that the best way to count our many blessings is to share them with others. That's why many Christians choose Lent as a perfect time to collect money, clothing, and other things for the poor. Children quickly enter into the spirit of such efforts.

Easter, of course, is the holiest day of the year for Christians, the victory of life over death. There's so much more to Easter than chocolate bunnies and fake plastic grass (essential as they are!). We invite you to adopt some of the prayers presented here to help deepen the meaning of Lent and Easter for your entire family.

Joyfully, this Easter day,
I kneel, a little child, to pray;
Jesus, who hath conquered death,

Teach me, with my every breath,
To praise and worship Thee.
—Sharon Banigan

Christ is risen. He is risen, indeed. Alleluia!
—Ancient Christian prayer

Jesus Christ is ris'n today, Alleluia!
Our triumphant holy day, Alleluia!
Who did once upon the cross, Alleluia!
Suffer to redeem our loss, Alleluia!
—Hymn by Charles Wesley

Purge me with hyssop; and I shall be clean; wash me,
and I shall be whiter than snow.
Make me to hear joy and gladness; that the bones which
thou hast broken may rejoice.
Hide thy face from my sins, and blot out all mine
iniquities.
Create in me a clean heart, O God; and renew a right
spirit within me.
—Psalm 51:7-10

Table Liturgy for the Feast of Easter Sunday

THE FAMILY STANDS in prayerful silence around the table,
upon which stand two unlighted candles. After a few moments, the father (or single parent) of the family begins.

FATHER: Blessed are You, Lord our God,
who raised up Jesus from the tomb
and has gathered all of us around this table.

MOTHER: As the light of God
overcame the darkness of death,
may these candles we now light
be for us a sign of the flame of life
that burns within our hearts.

(Candles are lighted.)

As these Easter candles
call us to the feast of this our table,
may the light of Christ,
call us to Your eternal Easter feast.
May these candles delight our eyes
and add splendor to our meal.

FATHER: With great joy,
we come to our Easter dinner
as we continue our celebration
of the ever-newness of the resurrection
of our Lord and Savior, Jesus Christ.
We rejoice in the resurrection of spring,
as birds, flowers and fields come alive
after the long sleep of winter.
May we, in this Easter Sunday meal,
share with them the great joy of life.
Let us pause and, in silence,
lift up our hearts to God
in gratitude for this holy Easter meal.

(Pause for silent prayer)

*(If there are guests present, Father should continue
with the following.)*

As our Risen Lord came as a guest
and ate with His disciples,
may we be grateful for the presence at our table
of our guests, [*names*],
who bring to our table the holy presence of God
and add to our celebration of this great and
 joyful feast.
May God bless them,
for together with the food of this feast,
they give us reason for joy.

MOTHER: May the taste of goodness in this food
be a promise of the eternal Easter meal
we shall all share together with our Risen Lord.
May this Easter dinner be a sacrament
of springtime, peace, and eternal happiness.
Alleluia, Alleluia!
May God's blessing rest upon this table
and each of us. Amen.

ALL: (*toast*) Happy Easter *or* A Blessed Easter!

Graces

Apart from bedtime devotions, no prayer is uttered more frequently than grace before a meal. There is something so palpable, so inherently sacramental, about sharing food that many of us who have relinquished other prayers have doggedly held on to this one moment of thanksgiving. Throughout the Gospels, Jesus is made known to his followers through the breaking of bread.

Saying grace is both an act of gratitude and an acknowledgment of our dependence on forces that are greater than we are. Though we eat to be refreshed and renewed, our contemporary way of life—with its driving pace and its fast-food habits—militates against any feeling of renewal. On the contrary, we live in the age of the Maalox Moment.

It would be wrong to condemn this situation as simply a matter of cultural decadence. The fact is that we are working longer hours to keep pace with the cost of living. We are attending night courses or dropping kids off at sporting events. Single parents are struggling to earn a living and at the same time to provide a nurturing environment for their children. The family meal is a rare thing nowadays, and we can't always control that. But when it is possible to sit down to a family meal, saying grace is a wonderful way to draw together for a moment and transcend our busyness and pre-occupations.

If you say only one form of grace before every meal and fear that it has become just a mumbled formality, why not add one or two other graces and vary them? We have assembled many beautiful and moving graces that have been composed over many centuries.

One common practice is to say a spontaneous prayer at mealtimes. This prayer may go beyond offering thanks for the meal: it can include thanks for the presence of guests and even pressing concerns that affect one or more members of the family. Some families make prayers before dinner more extensive. When we asked the well-known pastor and Christian writer Eugene Peterson about his family's prayer habits, he told us that before his children grew into adulthood and left home, "table prayers" were a wonderful custom in his house. Beginning before the food was cooked, the Petersons would gather at the table and pray. The prayers, spontaneous and heartfelt, would begin with the eldest and descend in age. "They would just start gathering the whole world into those prayers," Peterson recalls.

Just remember: if you pray before a meal, don't go on so long that the food ends up either burnt or stone cold!

Though it may be logical or comfortable for a parent to say the grace, we believe that children ought to be given regular opportunities to pray in their own voices and in their own words.

Many families enjoy holding hands during grace—a gesture that outwardly demonstrates an inward unity. For those who are musically gifted, there are a number of graces that have been set to familiar music and can be sung before the meal.

Another practice worth considering is saying a grace *after* the meal. This provides a wonderful sense of closure to the meal before everyone scatters to the four winds.

How about saying grace in public? We mentioned earlier that our daughter Magdalen found this distasteful. Most of us have an instinctive shyness about praying in public places, from McDonald's to a four-star restaurant: we don't want to seem ostentatious, as if we were flaunting our faith in front of others. It's a natural form of reticence, perhaps, but in an era that promotes self-expression as a high value, perhaps we should be unselfconscious enough to pray anywhere.

Finally, saying grace before a meal is the ideal time to think about those who are less fortunate. During penitential seasons like Advent and Lent, eating a little less can be linked to church- or community-related collections that give food to the poor.

GRACE BEFORE MEALS

Thank you for the world so sweet;
Thank you for the food we eat;
Thank you for the birds that sing;
Thank you, God, for everything.
    —E. Rutter Leatham

God, we thank you for this food,
For rest and home and all things good;
For wind and rain and sun above,
But most of all for those we love.
    —Maryleona Frost

God is great and God is good,
And we thank him for our food;
By his hand we must be fed,
Give us, Lord, our daily bread. Amen.
    —Anonymous

Bless, O Lord, this food to our use, and us to your
service.
    —Traditional grace

For what we are about to receive may the Lord make us
truly thankful. Amen.
    —Traditional grace

Be present at our table, Lord,
Be here and everywhere adored.

Thy creatures bless, and grant that we
May feast in paradise with thee.
   —John Wesley (may be sung to the
      tune of "The Old Hundredth")

For food and all Thy gifts of love,
We give Thee thanks and praise.
Look down, O Father, from above,
And bless us all our days. Amen.
   —Anonymous

Thou openest Thy hand, O Lord,
The earth is filled with good;
Teach us with grateful hearts to take
From Thee our daily food.
   —Anonymous

For health and food,
For love and friends,
For everything
Thy goodness sends,
Father in heaven,
We thank thee.
   —Ralph Waldo Emerson

We thank thee, Lord, for daily bread
As by thy hands our souls are fed.
Grant us to grow more like to thee,
Today and through eternity.
   —Anonymous

Come, Lord Jesus,
Be our Guest,
And let Thy gifts
To us be blessed. Amen.
—Anonymous

Bless Thou the work
that we have done,
Be it great or small;
On this, our food,
on us, each one,
Let now Thy blessing fall.
—Anonymous

LEADER: The eyes of all wait upon you.
RESPONSE: And you give them their meat in due season.
LEADER: You open your hand.
RESPONSE: And fill all living things with plenty.
LEADER We thank you, O Lord, for these your gifts,
(*or all*): and we beseech you to grant that whether we
eat or drink, or whatsoever we do, all may be
done to your glory. Amen.
—Traditional monastic grace
(derived from Psalm 145:15-16)

Our hands we fold,
Our heads we bow;
For food and drink
We thank Thee now.
—Anonymous

To God, who gives our daily bread,
A thankful song we'll raise,
And pray that he who sends our food
May fill our hearts with praise.
    —Thomas Tallis

The bread is pure and fresh,
the water is cool and clear.
Lord of all life, be with us,
Lord of all life, be near.
    —African grace

What God gives, and what we take,
'Tis a gift for Christ his sake:
Be the meal of beans and peas,
God be thanked for those, and these:
Have we flesh, or have we fish,
All are fragments from his dish.
    —Robert Herrick

O give thanks unto the Lord, for he is good; his mercy
endureth forever. He giveth food to all flesh; he giveth
to the beast his food, and to the young ravens which cry.
The Lord taketh pleasure in those that hope in his mercy.
    —Martin Luther

Let them thank the Lord for his steadfast love, for his
wonderful works to humankind. For he satisfies the
thirsty, and the hungry he fills with good things.
    —Psalm 107:8-9

Blessed art Thou, Lord our God, King of the universe, who in His goodness, grace, lovingkindness, and mercy, nourishes the whole world. He gives food to all flesh, for His lovingkindness is everlasting. In His great goodness, we have never lacked for food; may we never lack for food, for the sake of His great Name. For He nourishes and sustains all, He does good to all, and prepares food for all His creatures that He created. Blessed art Thou, Lord, who provides food for all.

    —*Birkat Hamazon,* Hebrew blessing for food

May the Merciful One bless the host and hostess and all who are seated about the table, just as our forefathers were blessed in every way with every manner of blessing.

    —Traditional Hebrew guest blessing

GRACE AFTER MEALS

Be known to us in breaking bread,
But do not *then* depart.
Savior abide with us and spread
Thy table in each heart.

    —Traditional German grace

Lord, you have fed us from your gifts and favors, fill us with your mercy, for you live and reign for ever and ever. Amen.

    —Ancient prayer from the Armenian
      Apostolic Church of Lebanon

May the abundance of this table never fail and never be less, thanks to the blessings of God, who has fed us and satisfied our needs. To him be glory forever. Amen.

—Ancient prayer from the Armenian
Apostolic Church of Lebanon

Lord, give all people the food they need, so that they may join us in giving you thanks. Amen.

—Anonymous

We thank you, our God,
for the food you have given us.
Make our sharing this bread together
lead to a renewal of our communion with you,
with one another, and with all creatures.
We ask this through Christ our Lord. Amen.

—Anonymous

SEASONAL GRACES

At Christmas

For this day of the dear Christ's birth, for its hours of home gladness and world gladness, for the love within these walls, which binds us together as a family, for our food on this table, for our surroundings in a land of freedom, we bring to Thee, our Father, our heartfelt gratitude. Bless all these, Thy favors, to our good, in Jesus' name. Amen

—H. B. Milward

At Easter

This day, O Christ, we celebrate Thy victory over death.
Bring to us new life of body through this nourishment,
and new life of soul by Thy presence with us now and
help us to say with Thy servant of old, "Thanks be to
God which giveth the victory through Jesus Christ our
Lord." Amen.

—From *Grace Before Meals,* compiled by
A. William Nyce and Hubert Bunyea

Thou hast given so much to me,
Give one thing more—a grateful heart;
Not thankful when it pleaseth me,
As if Thy blessings had spare days,
But such a heart whose pulse may be
Thy Praise.

—George Herbert

NATIONAL HOLIDAYS

WE HAVEN'T COME ACROSS MANY GRACES composed specif-
ically for national holidays, but there are prayers scattered
through this book that you might add to grace before your
evening meal—for example, a prayer from the section
"Work" on Labor Day or something relating to diversity or
social justice on Martin Luther King Jr. Day. However, the following prayers seemed appropriate for two of our national
holidays, and so we offer them here.

Independence Day

Bless our beautiful land, O Lord,
with its wonderful variety of people,
of races, cultures and languages.
May we be a nation
of laughter and joy,
of justice and reconciliation,
of peace and unity,
of compassion, caring and sharing.
We pray this prayer for a true patriotism,
in the powerful name of Jesus our Lord.

    —Archbishop Desmond Tutu

God, source of all freedom,
This day is bright with the memory
Of those who declared that life and liberty
Are your gift to every human being.
Help us to continue a good work begun long ago.
Make our vision clear and our will strong:
That only in human solidarity will we find liberty,
And justice only in the honor that belongs
To every life on earth.
Turn our hearts toward the family of nations:
To understand the ways of others,
To offer friendship,
And to find safety only in the common good of all.
We ask this through Christ our Lord. Amen.

    —*Catholic Household Blessings and Prayers*

Thanksgiving Day

Come ye thankful people, come,
Raise the song of harvest home:
All is safely gathered in,
Ere the winter storms begin;
God, our Maker, doth provide
For our wants to be supplied;
Come to God's own temple, come,
Raise the song of harvest home.
—Hymn by Henry Alford

Table Liturgy for Thanksgiving

THE FAMILY STANDS in prayerful silence around the table, upon which stand two unlighted candles. After a few moments, the mother (or single parent) of the family begins.

MOTHER: Come, let us welcome the feast of Thanksgiving
with joy and with light.
Light is the symbol of the divine.
The Lord is our light and our salvation.
May the light of gratitude burn brightly
in our hearts
and around this table,
not only on the feast of Thanksgiving
but at all meals.

(*Candles are lighted.*)

MOTHER   In the silence of our hearts,
(*or another*): let each of us give thanks
            for all the many gifts that are ours.

            (*Pause for silent reflection*)

            Let us also be mindful of those today
            who are without food and a home.

            (*Pause for silent reflection*)

MOTHER: And let us remember those whom we love
            who are not now present at our table.

            (*Pause for silent reflection*)

FATHER: Lord of Gifts,
            from Your holy heart
            has come a flood of gifts to us.
            With uplifted hearts, we have gathered around
            this table
            to thank You with prayer
            and with the worship of feasting.
            We are grateful
            not only for the gifts of life itself,
            but for all the gifts
            of friendship, love, devotion and forgiveness
            that we have shared.
            On this feast of giving thanks, Lord God,
            we thank You for showing us how to return
                thanks
            by lives of service,
            by deeds of hospitality,
            by kindness to a stranger
            and by concern for each other.

(If there are guests present, Father should continue with the following.)

We thank You for the presence of our guests
    [*names*],
who, by their being present in our home,
have added to the brightness of our celebration.
We are most grateful, this feast day,
for the way You, our hidden God,
have become visible to us
in one another,
in countless daily gifts
and in the marvels of creation.
Come, Lord of Gifts,
and bless our table and all the food of this feast.
Let us thank the Lord,
today and all days, Amen.

ALL: *(toast)* Happy Thanksgiving!
    —Edward Hays

Blessings

Many people assume that only a priest or minister can confer blessings on something or someone. There's no doubt that in many instances and traditions, it is utterly appropriate for an ordained minister to perform such actions—at baptisms, weddings, funerals, and many other ceremonies by which we celebrate key moments in our lives.

But it would be a mistake to assume that blessings can only be given by "official" representatives of religious communities. As we've suggested, parents can, and should, bless their children. To bless something is nothing more or less than to pronounce it good.

A question may naturally arise here: If something is self-evidently good, why should it need to be blessed? Our answer is simple: to put something into words, especially if it is said out loud, helps make it more real to us and to others who hear it. We should bless things for the same reason that we say to our parent or spouse or child "I love you." When we keep something bottled up inside us, it becomes abstract and distant. John Henry Newman once said that "faith follows action." By that he meant that we must embody our beliefs in concrete forms before they can be fully present to our minds and hearts.

Blessing, by the way, is the essence of Jewish prayer. According to Ariel Burger, "The Hebrew word *bracha* ["blessing"] is related to the word for pool of water, which in the desert meant life. For a people wandering in a spiritual desert, a pool of water can mean renewal and hope. Like water in the desert, a blessing is something miraculous, unfamiliar, unexpected." Burger explains that in Judaism, there are two forms of blessing, one that grows out of our encounter with the natural world and one that is based on our relationships to other people. "The first allows us to connect with and appreciate what is around us; the second allows us to give many gifts to the people around us."

Now don't get us wrong: we aren't advocating that families engage in some hyperactive effort to toss blessings around at the drop of a hat. Blessings seem to be called for only at special, appropriate times. For example, there is something fitting about blessing a house or an apartment shortly before or after one moves in. But when the appropriate times arrive, we ought not to be shy about blessing the things that give meaning to our lives.

The following blessings can be said on occasions such as moving into a home, getting a new pet, or taking leave of a visiting friend or relative. But they can also be added once in a while to your daily prayer time.

⌒

FOR THE HOME

Peace be to this house
And to all who dwell in it.
Peace be to those who enter
And to those who depart.
  —Anonymous

May God, the Father of goodness,
who commanded us to help one another
as brothers and sisters,
bless this building with his presence
and look kindly on all who enter here. Amen.
  —*Catholic Household Blessings and Prayers*

O God, protect our going out and our coming in;
let us share the hospitality of this home
with all who visit us,
that those who enter here may know your love and
    peace.
Grant this through Christ our Lord. Amen.
  —*Catholic Household Blessings and Prayers*

FRIENDS, NEIGHBORS, RELATIVES

God bless all the people I love,
God bless all the people who love me,
God bless all who love the people I love,
And all those who love the people who love me.
    —Based on an old New England sampler

May the road rise up to meet you,
may the wind be always at your back,
may the sun shine upon your face,
the rains fall soft upon your fields
and, until we meet again,
may God hold you in the palm of His hand.
    —Ancient Irish Blessing

The Lord bless you and keep you,
The Lord make his face to shine upon you and be
    gracious unto you;
The Lord lift up his countenance upon you and
give you peace.
    —Numbers 6:24–26

O Thou, who art the God of all the families of the earth;
we beseech Thee to bless all our friends and kindred,
wherever they may be, especially [*names*], and grant that
we may ever be knit together in bonds of mutual love.
    —Anonymous

Be gracious to all that are near and dear to me, and keep us all in your fear and love. Guide us, good Lord, and govern us by the same Spirit, that we may be so united to you here as not to be divided when you are pleased to call us hence, but may together enter into your glory, through Jesus Christ, our blessed Lord and Savior.

    —After John Wesley

O God of Love, we pray thee give us love: love in our thinking, love in our speaking, love in our doing, and love in the hidden places of our souls; love of our neighbors, near and far; love of our friends, old and new; love of those with whom we take our ease; love in joy, and love in sorrow; love in life, and love in death: that so at length we may be worthy to dwell with thee, who art Eternal Love.

    —Anonymous

PETS

Hear our prayer, O Lord, our God, who gives us all good things. Bless all animals and protect them from danger. We pray for the animals who are sick, lost, or starving. Animals are a wonderful part of this world, especially our pets. Please help us love them as you love us. Amen.

    —Helena Wolfe

Hear our humble prayer, O God, for our friends the animals. We entreat for them all thy mercy and pity,

and for those who deal with them we ask a heart
of compassion and gentle hands and kindly words.
Make us ourselves to be true friends to animals and
so to share the blessing of the merciful. For the sake
of thy Son, the tender-hearted, Jesus Christ our Lord.
  —Traditional Russian prayer

O God, source of life and power, Who feedeth the birds
of the heavens, increase our tenderness toward all the
creatures of Thy hand. Help us refrain from petty acts
of cruelty or thoughtless deeds of harm to any living
animal. May we care for them at all times, especially
during hard weather, and protect them from injury so
that they learn to trust us as friends. Let our sympathy
grow with knowledge so that all of creation may rejoice
in Thy presence.
  —Anonymous

FOR SAFE TRAVEL

PARTING, as the Bard has famously reminded us, is sweet sorrow. Whenever we travel, whether together as a family or with
parents and kids going off in different directions, there is a
certain emotional resonance that everyone feels. We may be
pulling out of the driveway for a summer vacation across the
country or just waving goodbye to Mom or Dad or a visiting
relative at the airport, but at these moments we are reminded
not only of our loves and but also of our vulnerabilities.

It seems only natural to mark these moments with prayer—
for good health and safety, for swift reunions and continued

blessings. Some Protestant Christians have a beautiful phrase
for this sort of prayer: they pray for "traveling mercies."

The light of God surrounds me;
The love of God enfolds me;
The power of God protects me;
The presence of God watches over me.
Wherever I am, God is.
    —James Dillet Freeman, "Prayer of Protection"

Alone with none but you, my God,
I journey on my way.
What need I fear, when you are near,
O King of night and day?
More safe am I within your hand
Than if a host did round me stand.
    —Saint Columba

Go before thy servant this day;
if Thou thyself go not forth with me,
carry me not up hence.
Thou, who didst guide the Israelites by an Angel,
the wise men by a star;
who didst preserve Peter in the waves,
and Paul in the shipwreck;
be present with me, O Lord, and dispose my way;
go with me, and lead me out, and lead me back.
    —Lancelot Andrewes

O Thou who art the confidence of the ends of the earth, and of them that are far off upon the sea, we commend to Thine Almighty protection all travelers by sea and land. Overshadow them with Thy mercy, and surround them with Thy love. When they cry in distress, do Thou mercifully send them help and deliverance. Go with them on their journey, and grant to those who are far from their homes that they might revisit them, in Thy good name, in peace.

—Anonymous

Births, Birthdays, and Siblings

What we call the "family" comes in a lot more sizes and shapes today than it did even a generation ago. And yet for all the changes that have taken place in our domestic lives, the essential meaning of "family" hasn't changed. Getting along with one's siblings is still just as hard as it ever was. That's why the family was once called the "school of charity," because learning to live with one another in a family calls on us to learn forbearance and forgiveness.

The birth of a child can be an emotional challenge for older children—even if some of those children are much older. We all want and need attention, and the arrival of a brother or sister can seem to threaten that. We've included prayers that deal with this sometimes tumultuous time.

Then there's the civil war that kids fight on a daily basis, which probably takes its biggest toll on Mom and Dad. Don't worry: we're not naïve enough to tell you that prayer will stop your kids from bickering and grousing. But our experience tells us that prayer—particularly evening prayer—gives children a chance to forgive and forget. That's not a miraculous cure, and it is almost always done "after the fact," but it helps them cultivate the habit of forgiveness. And we're convinced that over the course of years, that *does* make a huge difference.

⌒

Dear God, thank you for my baby [*brother/sister*].
Help me be a loving [*sister/brother*]. Help me understand that my baby [*brother/sister*] needs me even if all [*he/she*] wants to do all day is nurse and cry. I know that a baby needs to be hugged and kissed. Now that I am big, I understand why babies need so much attention from Mommy and Daddy. Help me remember that I was once little. Help me not get mad. Thank you for giving me this beautiful baby.
   —Suzanne M. Wolfe

Dear Lord, please help me be patient with my brothers and sister, especially when they trash my room and bug me with questions all the time. Help me understand what they need and who they are, even though I am so different from them. Help me love them as you love me—unconditionally and constantly like my Mom and Dad love me. Amen.
   —Magdalen Wolfe

God made the sun
And God made the tree,
God made the mountains
And God made me.
   —Anonymous

Thank you, Lord, for this special day. Thank you for
the cake and the candles and the presents. All of these
things tell me that I am special. But most of all, thank
you for the love of my Mommy and Daddy and [*names
of brothers and sisters*].
   —Suzanne M. Wolfe

O loving God, today is my birthday.
For your care from the day I was born until today
and for your love, I thank you.
Help me be strong and healthy,
and help me show love for others, as Jesus did.
   —Prayer from Japan

My Father, all last year you took care of me and now
you have given me a birthday. I thank you for all your
goodness and kindness to me. You have given me loving
parents, a home, gifts, and clothes. Thank you, God.
Help me to be a better child in my new year—to grow
strong, to study well, to work happily.
   —Prayer from India

But now thus says the Lord, he who created you.
Do not fear, for I have redeemed you; I have called
   you by name, you are mine.
   —Isaiah 43:1

Birthday Blessing Prayer for a Child

Lord our God,
Not only [*name*] but each of us
Rejoices in this birthday
Because birthdays are among the best
Of all our family feasts.
Today we celebrate that [*name*]
Has been Your gift to all of us,
A gift that grows more valuable in our hearts
With each passing day.
Bless [*her/him*] on this [*her/his number*] birthday
With blessings of good health,
Of laughter and happiness.
On this birthday, may [*her/his*] heart overflow
With good things and beautiful dreams.
Lord, Holy Creator of Fun and Song,
Come and join us now as we wish [*name*]
A happy birthday as we sing:
(*All sing "Happy Birthday."*)
    —Edward Hays

Coming-of-Age Prayers

When our eldest child, Magdalen, became a teenager, we suddenly felt as if we had to learn how to be parents all over again. Like countless parents before us, we found ourselves turning to one another and saying, "Just when we thought we were getting good at this . . ."

So we step out onto the dance floor and try to master the new and intricate movements that now seem required of us. Magdalen, the child-woman, struggled for independence, tested the limits of her freedom, and coped with the hormones that began to surge inside her. We found ourselves stepping on each other's toes and trying not to lose our tempers. How to keep that precarious balance between the expressions of our unconditional love and the need to set boundaries?

Adolescence is also the time when everything is called into question, *especially* the beliefs and habits of adults. One of the most disconcerting aspects of adolescence is the extent to which the child draws a veil over her inner life. What once was transparent has become opaque. The temptation for the parent is to try to reach inside and find out what's going on, but that can't be done without violating the child's privacy and developing conscience. Sometimes the most important way to demonstrate love for a teen is to show respect for that private inner life.

Adolescence is a difficult but necessary period of adjustment. It can also be profoundly rewarding, as we learn to relate to our children on a more adult level. We've included prayers that would be appropriate when children are preparing for and then experiencing the rite of Confirmation. These prayers are included not only to help mark this ceremony but also because they signify a child's coming of age.

⌒

Be thou a bright flame before me,
Be thou a guiding star above me,
Be thou a smooth path below me,
Be thou a kindly shepherd behind me,
Today—tonight—and for ever.
   —Saint Columba

Lord, how glad we are that we don't hold you but
that you hold us.
   —Prayer from Haiti

Lord, I want to go where You want me to go,
Do what You want me to do,
Be what You want me to be.
Save me!
   —American spiritual

Holy God who madest me
And all things else to worship thee,
Keep me fit in mind and heart,
Body and soul, to take my part.
Fit to stand and fit to run,
Fit for sorrow, fit for fun,
Fit for work and fit for play,
Fit to face life day by day.
Holy God, who madest me,
Make me fit to worship thee.
   —Bishop R. Mant

I am yours, I was born for you;
what is your will for me?
Let me be rich or beggared,
exulting or lamenting,
comforted or lonely;
since I am yours, yours only,
what is your will for me?
   —Saint Teresa of Avila

School

Outside of the home, the dominant influence on a child's life is usually her experience at school. Both as a place of learning and as the central location for your child's "socialization," school is the place where children have to begin to make their way in the world without immediate support from their parents. From the day we drop our kids off at preschool or kindergarten to the day they graduate from college, our kids enter a microcosm of society itself. Indeed, school might be likened to a theatrical stage on which a young person begins to test and shape her character. On this stage, many triumphs and tragedies are enacted. Here a child encounters the realities of academic and athletic competition, peer pressure, all the anxieties and pleasures of social life, and the mysterious fact that boys and girls are intriguingly different from one another.

You don't have to be a proponent of prayer in the public schools to see that there are times when children might benefit from putting their joys and sadnesses into the context of prayer. We have found in our own home that children frequently come back from school with emotional stresses and strains that they need to work out, even if they're too shy to approach such issues directly.

As many of the great writers have demonstrated—think of Charlotte Brontë's *Jane Eyre* or Charles Dickens's *Nicholas Nickleby*, for example—children have a keen and finely tuned sense of justice. If a teacher or a fellow student has been harsh or indifferent, a child's heart can be sorely wounded. One of the glories of childhood, of course, is that children seem capable of forgiving and forgetting with breathtaking ease. But at the same time, they need to get things out in the open. Prayer offers them the perfect opportunity to unburden themselves and move on with their lives.

Our kids are eager to share their achievements and joys with us—if we make the time to listen to them. Prayer provides at least one moment in the day (although it shouldn't be the only one) when our kids can give thanks in our presence for those special triumphs.

The prayers we've gathered here relate primarily to the academic and athletic challenges of attending school, but there will be times when a child's experience at school—from physical and emotional injuries to learning disabilities—might lead you to seek out prayers from other sections of this book. While it would be wrong for us as parents to be overly intrusive about our kids' experiences at school, there are moments when we can give children a prayerful context in order to work through difficulties and challenges.

～

Lord of wisdom, who gives us minds and hearts to know and love your creation, make us eager to learn, patient with our mistakes and failures, and quick to forgive schoolmates who have been unfair to us, so that we use our knowledge to build a better world. Amen.
—Gregory Wolfe

Holy Spirit, help us in this school, to live together in love and peace and to be patient with each other's faults and mindful of each other's wants. May we be gentle in words and helpful in deeds, not seeking our own profit only but rather the good of all. Fill our hearts and minds so completely with thy presence that they may compel us to love one another.
—Anonymous

From the cowardice that dare not face new truth
From the laziness that is contented with half-truth
From the arrogance that thinks it knows all truth,
Good Lord, deliver me.
—Prayer from Kenya

Grant, O Lord, to all teachers and students, to know
what is worth knowing, to love what is worth loving,
to praise what pleases you most, and to dislike what is
evil in your eyes. Grant us true judgment to distinguish
things that differ and above all to search out and to do
what is pleasing to you; through Jesus Christ our Lord.

—After Thomas à Kempis

O Lord, who is the fountain of all wisdom and learning,
you have given me the years of my youth to learn the
arts and skills necessary for an honest and holy life.
Enlighten my mind, that I may acquire knowledge.
Strengthen my memory, that I may retain what I have
learnt. Govern my heart, that I may always be eager
and diligent in my studies. And let your Spirit of truth,
judgment and prudence guide my understanding, that
I may perceive how everything I hear fits into your holy
plan for the world.

—John Calvin

Work

Most parents, it seems safe to say, want their children to achieve success in life, however variously the word *success* might be defined. We urge our children to do well in school, send them to music lessons, and sign them up for martial arts classes and soccer teams. Then we attend their recitals or follow their bus around for hundreds of miles to cheer them on to victory.

Is it possible that in the past decade or two, parents have become a little obsessed about urging their children to *perform* in one way or another? When we watch a movie like *Parenthood*, we laugh at the absurdity of the Rick Moranis character, who drills his child day and night in order to turn her into an intellectual prodigy—a child who is all head but no heart.

When we make demands of our children, are we seeking what is best for them or somehow trying to live vicariously through them? How do we draw the line between instilling good habits—a "work ethic," if you will—and letting them enjoy the wonderful leisure of childhood?

Obviously, there are no simple answers to these questions. Every parent has to struggle to find the golden mean between extremes. But there is no denying that children must learn to work, whether that work is merely the simple math problems of a third grader or the daily household chores or the pocket-money jobs of adolescence.

Because the work we do reveals who we are and what we care about, it is important that children understand that their efforts have a deeper meaning. If we make work into mere drudgery or a concerted effort to achieve stardom and success, we impoverish our own lives as well as those of our children. To pray about the various kinds of work we undertake is to place those efforts in a larger context. A Hebrew phrase helps Jews define their mission on earth: *tikkun olam,* "repairing the world." Children need to see their work as part of a larger human effort to repair, clean, and build up the world. So do grown-ups.

The prayers featured here can be said before embarking on any kind of work, whether that be school, a paper route, or a summer job. Labor Day would be another appropriate time to say prayers relating to work. Or they can just be added on occasion to your daily prayers when you want to focus for a moment on the meaning and value of work.

⌒

O Lord! you know how busy I must be this day:
if I forget you, please do not forget me.
—After Sir Jacob Astley

The things, good Lord, that I pray for, give me the
grace to labor for.
—Saint Thomas More

Be my guide, O Lord, I pray,
Lest I stumble on my way.
Be my strength, dear Lord, I ask,
That I may fulfill each task.
Teach me, my God and King,
In all things thee to see,
And what I do in anything
To do it as for thee.
—George Herbert

O Lord, help me to understand that you ain't going
to let nothing come my way that You and me together
can't handle.
—Anonymous African boy, quoted
    by Marian Wright Edelman

My God, you are always close to me. In obedience to
you, I must now apply myself to outward things. Yet,
as I do so, I pray that you will give me the grace of your
presence. And to this end I ask that you will assist my
work, receive its fruits as an offering to you, and all
the while direct all my affections to you.
—Brother Lawrence

Lord Jesus,
take my mind and think through me,
take my hands and bless through me,
take my mouth and speak through me,
take my spirit and pray in me;
above all, Lord Jesus,
take my heart and love through me,
so that it is you who live and work in me.
　　—After Lancelot Andrewes

Lord, in union with your love, unite my work with
your great work, and perfect it. As a drop of water,
poured into a river, is taken up into the activity of the
river, so may my labor become part of your work. Thus
may those among whom I live and work be drawn into
your love.
　　—Saint Gertrude the Great

Lord, when you call us to live and work for you,
give us the wisdom to remember
that it is not the beginning
but the faithful continuing of the task
that is most important in your eyes,
until we have completed it to the best of our ability.
　　—After Sir Francis Drake

God of work and rest and pleasure,
grant that what we do this week may be for us
an offering rather than a burden;
and for those we serve, may it be the help they need.
　　—*A New Zealand Prayer Book*

Give me, dear Lord, a pure heart and a wise mind, that I may carry out my work according to your will. Save me from all false desires, from pride, greed, envy and anger, and let me accept joyfully every task you set before me. Let me seek to serve the poor, the sad and those unable to work. Help me to discern honestly my own gifts that I may do the things of which I am capable, and happily and humbly leave the rest to others. Above all, remind me constantly that I have nothing except what you give me, and can do nothing except what you enable me to do.

—Jacob Boehme

Illness and
Times of Need

When Greg was a boy, he suffered from asthma and recurrent bouts of bronchitis—illnesses that he had inherited from his father. Living as he did on Long Island, with its high humidity and pollen counts, he was frequently confined to bed for days on end.

Back in the 1960s, before the advent of preventive treatments and over-the-counter inhalers, asthma medicine was taken from a nebulizer made of intricate glass tubing and rubber. You poured the liquid medicine—a straight shot of adrenaline, more or less—into the nebulizer, placed it in your mouth, squeezed it, and inhaled. Then your heart would race with adrenaline and the passages in your lungs would open up for a while. But even then the bronchitis made it hard to breathe as Greg's chest filled with phlegm and the coughing never seemed to end.

Nights were the worst times. Even with long naps, the effort of coughing all day took its toll. Being tired and yet unable to sleep was not easy for an eight-year-old to deal with. His mother lovingly cared for him during the day, and his father would come home from work and sit by Greg's bedside at night. The fact that Greg's illness was inherited from his father created a bond that somehow made the suffering easier to bear.

But what Greg remembers from those nights was the scripture passages and prayers that his father intoned in a quiet but soothingly rhythmic voice. The Gospel of John was Greg's dad's favorite. "In the beginning was the Word, and the Word was with God, and the Word was God." "Let not your hearts be troubled; believe in God, believe also in me. In my Father's house are many rooms; if it were not so, would I have told you that I go to prepare a place for you?"

There's no doubt in Greg's mind that it was the tone of his father's voice, even more than the content, that was so profoundly comforting. But would that voice have been as comforting if it had not been beseeching God for a boy's healing?

It has been said that prayer is love in action. When our children are ill or suffering from some sadness or distress, should we not demonstrate our love by praying for, with, and *over* them?

The King of love my Shepherd is,
Whose goodness faileth never
I nothing lack if I am his
And he is mine forever.
   —Henry Williams Baker

O God our Father, bless all who suffer and give them
courage, strength and peace.
Amen.
   —John G. Williams

When I am afraid, I put my trust in you.
   —Psalm 56:3

Bless all the children in hospitals. Help them to
   grow stronger every day
and to be happy, cheerful and patient. Be with all
   the ill people everywhere.
Help them to know that Thou art with them and
   art taking care of them.
   —Bertha C. Krall

Why should I feel discouraged?
Why should the shadows fall?
Why should my heart feel lonely
and long for heaven and home?
When Jesus is my portion
A constant friend is he.
His eye is on the sparrow
And I know he watches me.

I sing because I'm happy,
I sing because I'm free.
His eye is on the sparrow
And I know he watches me.
    —American spiritual

I believe in the sun even when it is not shining.
I believe in love even when feeling it not.
I believe in God even when he is silent.
    —Jewish prayer

Father of mercy,
Lover of all children,
Who in their form didst send Thy Son;
Gladly we bless thee,
Humbly we pray thee,
For all the children of the earth.
In thy compassion,
Helper of the helpless,
Tend them in sickness, ease their pain,
Heal their diseases,
Lighten their sorrows,
And from all evil keep them free.
    —Silesian hymn

Precious Lord, take my hand.
Lead me on. Help me stand.
I am tired. I am weak. I am worn.
Through the storm,
Through the night,

Lead me on to the light.
Take my hand, precious Lord,
Lead me home.

    —American spiritual

Hear my prayer, O Lord, and let my cry come unto
    thee.
Hide not thy face from me in the day when I am
    in trouble;
incline thine ear unto me: in the day when I call
    answer me speedily.
My days are like a shadow that declineth;
and I am withered like grass.
But thou, O Lord, shalt endure for ever;
and thy remembrance unto all generations.

    —Psalm 102:1–2, 11–12

The Lord sustains them on their sickbed; in their illness
you heal all their infirmities.

    —Psalm 41:3

O Lord our God
and God of our fathers!
Mercifully direct and guide our steps
to our destination,
and let us arrive there
in health, joy and peace!
Keep us from snares and dangers,
and protect us from any enemies
that we might meet along the way.

    —Ancient Jewish prayer

Dear God, be good to me:
Thy sea is so wide, and my boat is so small.
  —Prayer of the Breton Fishermen

I am here abroad,
I am here in need,
I am here in pain,
I am here in straits,
I am here alone.
O God, aid me.
  —Celtic Prayer

Save us, O God,
for your mercy's sake.
Protect us from our enemies
and keep far from us
evil and conflict,
hunger and affliction.
Keep us from stumbling
and falling into danger.
Shelter us in the shadow of your wings,
for you are our protection and salvation;
goodness and mercy are yours.
Watch over our going out and coming in.
Spread over us your mantle of peace.
  —Part of a blessing recited on the evening of
    the Sabbath and of festivals, after the Sh'ma

Send down your angel
who in his mercy gives comfort and relief
to those who suffer.
Let the sick and infirm be healed.
Lighten and relieve their pain.
Let them have respite from their suffering
that they may see your light.
Let healing come swiftly with the dawn.
Blessed are you, O Lord,
who uphold the sick on their bed of sorrow!
May their days once more be good
and their years happy!
Blessed are you
who uphold, save and restore the sick.

    —Ancient Jewish prayer

Heal us, O Lord, and we shall be healed,
Save us and we shall be saved,
For Thou art our glory.
Send complete healing for our every illness,
For Thou, Divine King, art the faithful, merciful
    Physician.
Blessed are Thou, Lord, who heals the sick of
    His people Israel.

    —*Refuah,* Hebrew blessing

Tend thy sick ones, O Lord Christ,
rest thy weary ones.
Bless thy dying ones.
Soothe thy suffering ones.
Pity thy afflicted ones.
And all for thy love's sake.

   —Saint Augustine

I will lift up mine eyes unto the hills, from whence
    cometh my help.
My help cometh from the Lord, which made heaven
    and earth.
He will not suffer thy foot to be moved: he that
    keepeth thee will not slumber.
Behold, he that keepeth Israel shall neither slumber
    nor sleep.
The Lord is thy keeper: The Lord is thy shade upon
    thy right hand.
The sun shall not smite thee by day, nor the moon
    by night.
The Lord shall preserve thee from all evil: he shall
    preserve thy soul.
The Lord shall preserve thy going out and thy coming
    in from this time forth, and even for evermore.

   —Psalm 121

O God, who knowest us to be set in the midst of so many and great dangers, that by reason of the frailty of our nature we cannot always stand upright; grant to us such strength and protection, as may support us in all dangers, and carry us through all temptations; through Jesus Christ our Lord.

—*Book of Common Prayer*

When Someone Dies

Suzanne will never forget one day when she took our first-born, Magdalen, out shopping. Magdalen was just two at the time. It was spring, and as they walked along the main street of the small town where we lived, Suzanne spotted someone selling balloons. "*Boons!*" Magdalen cried. Suzanne bought her one and tied it to her wrist so it wouldn't fly off. The rest of the afternoon Magdalen gravely watched it bob and twist in the air above her head. Her delight in it, as with most toddlers, was solemn and intense.

Then it was time to go home. When they got to the car, Magdalen insisted on holding the string to the balloon in her hand. Without thinking, Suzanne opened one of the windows because the afternoon had turned very warm and the air-conditioning in the car didn't work. A few minutes later, while Suzanne was driving down the highway, she heard a heart-wrenching wail. Looking in the rear-view mirror, she saw that the balloon had slipped out of Magdalen's fingers and disappeared through the window. Magdalen was craning her neck to watch it soar away up into the sky. Her grief was enormous, and there was little that Suzanne could do to console her.

That day Suzanne realized that even the smallest child can suffer the most intense pain of loss. Whether it is a favorite stuffed animal that finally comes apart, a beloved blanket that shreds in the washer, or a cherished pet that dies, the loss is a type of death. A child's grief, like his joy, has a burning purity that seems to blot out everything else.

So it is when a friend or family member dies. If adults have a difficult time coming to terms with death, how can a child, bursting with youth and energy, understand the mystery of human mortality? To complicate matters further, our culture has such an aversion to death that many critics have written about death being the "final taboo" in contemporary society.

How you decide to console your child when someone near to you dies will depend on your own particular blending of faith and psychological wisdom. It is one thing to speak of Christ's resurrection and the existence of heaven, but how does one speak of such things without somehow sounding a hollow note?

What we have discovered in our family is that the long, slow process of grieving seems to stall without the aid of prayer. Because those who die depart from us, there is a basic human instinct to send our prayers after them and their families. In prayer, we cherish the memories of those whom we have loved, and we come to a deeper understanding of the preciousness of every human life.

T. S. Eliot, who composed many poems that were at the same time prayers, once wrote that "love is most nearly itself when here and now cease to matter." In a similar vein, as it says in the Song of Solomon, "love is as strong as death." Neither children nor adults will ever completely fathom the mystery of death, but when we focus our love for those who have passed on into prayer, we come as close to understanding death as it is humanly possible to do.

⌒

Lord Jesus, receive [*name*]'s spirit.
  —Adapted from Acts 7:59

God be in my head, and in my understanding;
God be in my eyes, and in my looking;
God be in my mouth, and in my speaking;
God be in my heart, and in my thinking;
God be at my end, and at my departing.
  —*Sarum Primer*

All shall be well,
and all shall be well,
and all manner of things shall be well.
  —Julian of Norwich

Eternal rest grant unto them, O Lord, and may perpetual light shine upon them. May they rest in peace. Amen.
  —Ancient Christian prayer

Let nothing disturb thee,
Nothing affright thee;
All things are passing;
God never changeth;
Patience endurance
Attaineth to all things;
Who God possesseth
In nothing is wanting;
Alone God sufficeth.
—Saint Teresa of Avila

Blessed are they that mourn: for they shall be comforted.
—Matthew 5:4

Into Thy hands, Lord, I commend my spirit:
Thou hast redeemed me, O Lord God of truth.
—Psalm 31:5

Abide with me: fast falls the eventide;
The darkness deepens; Lord, with me abide;
When other helpers fail, and comforts flee,
Help of the helpless, O abide with me.
—Henry Francis Lyte, "Eventide"

Bring us, O Lord, at our last awakening
into the house and gate of heaven,
to enter into that gate and dwell in that house
where shall be no darkness nor dazzling,
but one equal light;
no noise nor silence, but one equal music;
no fears nor hopes, but one possession;

no ends nor beginnings, but one equal eternity
in the habitations of your glory and dominion,
world without end.

    —John Donne

Give rest, O Christ, to your servants, with your saints,
where sorrow and pain are no more, neither sighing,
but life everlasting.

    —Russian Orthodox *Kontakion of the Departed*

Thy might is eternal, O Lord,
Who revives the dead,
Powerful in saving,
Who makes the wind to blow and the rain to fall,
Who sustains the living with loving kindness,
Who revives the dead with great mercy,
Who supports the falling, heals the sick, frees
    the captive,
And keeps faith with the dead;
Who is like Thee, Almighty, and who resembles Thee,
O King who can bring death and give life,
And can make salvation blossom forth.
And faithful art Thou to revive the dead.
Blessed art Thou, Lord, who makes the dead live.

    —*Gevurot,* Hebrew blessing

O God, your Son chose the path which led to pain before
joy and the cross before glory. Plant his cross in our
hearts, so that in its power and love we may come at last
to joy and glory; through your Son, Jesus Christ our Lord.

    —*Lutheran Book of Worship*

The Lord is my shepherd; I shall not want.
He maketh me to lie down in green pastures:
he leadeth me beside the still waters.
He restoreth my soul: he leadeth me in the
paths of righteousness for his name's sake.
Yea, though I walk through the valley of the
shadow of death, I will fear no evil: for thou
art with me; thy rod and thy staff they comfort me.
Thou preparest a table before me in the
presence of mine enemies: thou anointest
my head with oil; my cup runneth over.
Surely goodness and mercy shall follow me all
the days of my life: and I will dwell in the
house of the Lord for ever.

   —Psalm 23

Lead, kindly Light, amid the encircling gloom,
Lead thou me on;
The night is dark, and I am far from home,
Lead thou me on.
Keep thou my feet; I do not ask to see
The distant scene; one step enough for me.
I was not ever thus, nor prayed that thou
Shouldst lead me on;
I loved to choose and see my path; but now
Lead thou me on.
I loved the garish day, and in spite of fears,
Pride ruled my will: remember not past years.
So long thy power hath blest me, sure it still
Will lead me on.

O'er moor and fen, o'er crag and torrent, till
The night is gone,
And with the morn those Angel faces smile,
Which I have loved long since, and lost awhile.
  —John Henry Newman "Lead, Kindly Light"

O Father, give my spirit power to climb
To the fountain of all light, and be purified.
Break through the mists of earth, the weight of clay,
Shine forth in splendor, you who are calm weather,
And quiet resting-place for faithful souls.
You carry us, and you go before;
You are the journey, and the journey's end.
  —Boethius

A FAMILY LITURGY AFTER
SOMEONE HAS DIED

Opening Responses

Come among us, God.
You who cast the planets into space
and cradle the sparrow in her nest.
Come God and meet us here.
Come among us, God.
You who bless the poor and the broken
and stand by the sad and the strong.
Come God and meet us here.
Come among us, God.
You who dance in the silence
and shine in the darkness.
Come God and meet us here.

Readings

Psalm 139:7–10

Revelation 21:3–4

John 14:1–3

Space to Remember

THIS TIME MAY BE DEVOTED to remembering the person who has died. Here it would be appropriate to tell stories, sing songs, share common memories, bring into the present the things that we want to recall, and share silence. Use a ritual action that is meaningful to those present—for example, light a candle, place a stone or flower on a grave, float petals in water, place centrally something that recalls the departed.

All our laughter, all our sadness,
Safe now in God's hands.
All our anger, all our gladness,
Safe now in God's hands.
All our stories, all our memories,
Safe now in God's hands.
Those we remember, those we love,
Safe now in God's hands.

(Sing a song or listen to some favorite music.)

Closing Responses

We ask for the love of God
and the messages of angels.

The laughter of Jesus
and the stories of the saints.
The power of the spirit
and the strong hands of friends.
To bless us on life's journey
and lead us safely home, Amen.

—Ruth Burgess

Giving Thanks

When a toddler names the things around her, she isn't just stating the facts; she's making an exclamation. Doggy! Moon! Flower! Mommy! More often than not, when she utters these names, she will have a look on her face that seems to say, "You're noticing this, right? You're paying attention? Can you believe this?" Of course, if you fail to take sufficient notice, you're likely to feel a small hand grabbing your chin and yanking your head around in the right direction to allow you the chance to demonstrate the proper amazement. Only after you have shown the appropriate amount of reverence will the little taskmaster leave you in peace.

A child's capacity for wonder takes the stuff of everyday life and transforms it into the miraculous. Are the children wrong about this? By nature, children are theologians, not scientists, and they believe that the universe was made for them. If that is true, then it makes all the difference in the world as to how we ought to think and act. Children tell us— in no uncertain terms—that the cosmos is a gift that has been given to each and every one of us.

And the natural human reaction to a gift is to feel gratitude and to return thanks. Each exclamation out of the mouth of the toddler is simultaneously a shout of thanks. The simplest prayers for small children are almost always thank-you prayers: "Thank you for Mommy, Daddy, Grandma, Granddad," and so on.

Precisely because the prayer of thanksgiving comes so readily to the lips of a child, we may be tempted to think that it is the easiest and least demanding sort of prayer. But we're not sure that's true. From adolescence onward, it gets harder and harder for us to cultivate hearts that resonate with gratitude. Indeed, it is hard to believe that the effort to maintain a grateful heart is any less difficult, or less costly, than the effort needed to offer praise, seek forgiveness, or any of the other common modes of prayer. We get so caught up in our own concerns and schemes that we make the mistake of thinking that we are the source of all that is good in our lives. We forget how dependent we are on others, how much of what we have is pure gift.

The sin of ingratitude may not get that much publicity— it's not among the Seven Deadlies—but much grief comes in its wake. Shakespeare based what many consider his greatest tragedy, *King Lear*, on the theme of ingratitude. Without a grateful heart, it is all too easy to take things for granted or just to trash them and throw them away. It is nearly impossible to consistently abuse something that you feel grateful for. Will children vandalize, steal, or commit violence against persons and institutions for which they are thankful? Would they put their own bodies at risk through drugs, sexual promiscuity, and violence if they felt truly grateful for the gift of life?

There are millions of people around the world who have far less to be thankful for than they should. For those of us who have a superabundance of blessings, our gratitude should spur us on to what, spiritually speaking, is the next step: sharing our abundance with others.

⌒

All good gifts around us
Are sent from heaven above;
Then thank the Lord,
O thank the Lord,
For all his love.
   —Hymn by Matthias Claudius

May God give us grateful hearts
And keep us mindful
Of the needs of others.
   —Anonymous

Lord, you have given me so much; I ask for one more thing—a grateful heart.
   —After George Herbert

O give thanks to the Lord, for he is good;
his steadfast love endures forever!
I was pushed hard, so that I was falling,
but the Lord helped me.
You are my God, and I will give thanks to you;
you are my God, I will extol you.
    —Psalm 118:1, 13, 28

For all that has been—Thanks!
For all that shall be—Yes!
    —Dag Hammarskjöld

O God, I thank Thee for all the joy I have had in life.
    —Earl Brihtnoth, A.D. 991

Make a joyful noise to the Lord, all the earth.
Worship the Lord with gladness;
come into his presence with singing.
    —Psalm 100:1-2

Lord, behold our family here assembled.
We thank you for this place in which we dwell,
for the love that unites us,
for the peace accorded to us this day,
for the hope with which we expect the morrow;
for the health, the work, the food and the bright skies
that make our lives delightful;
for our friends in all parts of the earth. Amen.
    —Robert Louis Stevenson

O Father of goodness,
We thank you, each one,
For happiness, healthiness,
Friendship and fun,
For good things we think of
And good things we do,
And all that is beautiful,
Loving and true.
　　—Prayer from France

Now thank we all our God with hearts and hands
　　and voices,
Who wondrous things has done, in whom this
　　world rejoices;
Who, from our mothers' arms, has blessed us on
　　our way,
With countless gifts of love, and still is ours today.
O may this gracious God through all our life be
　　near us,
With ever joyful hearts and blessed peace to cheer us;
Preserve us in this grace, and guide us in distress,
And free us from all sin, till heaven we possess.
　　—Martin Rinkart

If my lips could sing as many songs
as there are waves in the sea:
if my tongue could sing as many hymns
as there are ocean billows:
if my mouth
filled the whole firmament with praise:

if my face
shone like the sun and moon together:
if my hands
were to hover in the sky like powerful eagles
and my feet
ran across mountains as swiftly as the deer;
all that would not be enough
to pay you fitting tribute,
O Lord my God.

    —Hymn probably composed in the
      Talmudic period, third to fifth century A.D.

Praise

The form of prayer that has traditionally gone under the name of praise is often mentioned in the same breath as that of thanksgiving. Both types of prayer grow out of our loving response to the gifts we have been given and the mystery and wonder of the world in which we live. But if thanksgiving leads us to focus on the gifts we enjoy, praise calls us to turn our thoughts toward God, the giver of every good gift. For that reason, most of the theologians, poets, and mystics who have written on prayer place praise on a somewhat higher plane than thanksgiving. Praise is more vertical: it leads us away from our own concerns and reaches up toward the divine.

But it is precisely this focus on God that makes praise just a bit more complicated for some people. Praise really requires you to decide what you believe about God. After all, in order to praise someone or something, you have to know a little about the qualities you are singling out for commendation. In our own family experience, we've noticed that we're a bit shy about offering spontaneous praise to God. And yet when we play a CD of Handel's *Messiah,* we're not averse to joining in lustily to his famous "Hallelujah" chorus. Similarly, there are plenty of psalms that we enjoy praying, each of which is a passionate and rollicking catalogue of praise to God. "Praise him with trumpet sound; praise him with lute and harp! Praise him with tambourine and dance; praise him with strings and pipe! Let everything that breathes praise the Lord!" (Psalm 150:3-4, 6a).

One thing we have discovered about praise, in spite of our shyness, is that it can bring with it a mysterious sense of liberation—an opportunity to lose oneself in the joyous celebration of God's goodness and love. Here the wisdom of the spiritual masters is made manifest: when you lose yourself in lifting up your thoughts to God, when you seek to become more Christlike, you can rediscover your innermost heart and thus be more truly yourself.

Children lead the way in teaching us about praise. No words are more thrilling to a parent than hearing a child say, "You're the best Mom/Dad in the whole wide world!" Children are unstinting with their praise, even if the words they use are less than churchly. In a child's mouth, "Cool!" and "Wow!" often say the same thing as "Alleluia" and "Gloria in excelsis."

A few years ago, Greg took up astronomy as a hobby, and he has taken the kids out stargazing a number of times. Ever since he was a child himself, Greg has found the glory of the night sky a sight that evokes his own wordless form of praise. Being able to point out the constellations, the rings of Saturn, and the fuzzy greenish haze that is the whirling Andromeda galaxy has been a delight for everyone—a chance to place ourselves in a praiseful mood. The psalmists loved to use the grandeur of nature as a springboard for prayer as they envisioned mountains and hills leaping like mountain goats in an ecstatic vision of the cosmos offering up praise to its Maker. Praise calls us out of ourselves and enables us to rejoice in childlike wonder.

⌒

Let the peoples praise you, O God;
let all the peoples praise you.
  —Psalm 67:3

Praise God from whom all blessings flow;
Praise Him, all creatures here below;
Praise Him above, ye heavenly host;
Praise Father, Son, and Holy Ghost.
  —Bishop Ken

I shall sing a praise to God;
Strike the chords upon the drum.
God who gives us all good things—
Strike the chords upon the drum.
  —Prayer from the Congo

Rejoice evermore.
Pray without ceasing.
In every thing give thanks.
    —1 Thessalonians 5:16-18

Let us with a gladsome mind
Praise the Lord for he is kind;
For his mercies shall endure,
Ever faithful, ever sure.
All things living he doth feed,
His full hand supplies their need:
For his mercies shall endure,
Ever faithful, ever sure.
    —John Milton

Let all the world in every corner sing
My God and King!
The heavens are not too high,
His praise may thither fly:
The earth is not too low,
His praises there may grow.
Let all the world in every corner sing
My God and King!
    —George Herbert

God,
to whom all hearts are open,
to whom all wills speak
and from whom no secret is hidden,
I beg you,

so as to cleanse the intent of my heart
with the unutterable gift of your grace,
that I may perfectly love you
and worthily praise you.
  —*The Cloud of Unknowing*

Praise to the Holiest in the height,
And in the depth be praise,
In all his words most wonderful,
Most sure in all his ways.
  —John Henry Newman

You are holy, Lord, the only God,
and your deeds are wonderful.
You are love, you are wisdom.
You are humility, you are endurance.
You are rest, you are peace.
You are joy and gladness.
You are all our riches, and you suffice for us.
You are beauty, you are gentleness.
You are our protector,
You are our guardian and defender.
You are courage,
You are our haven and hope.
You are our faith, our great consolation.
You are our eternal life, great and wonderful Lord,
God almighty, merciful Savior.
  —Saint Francis of Assisi

Praise ye the Lord. Praise ye the Lord from the heavens:
praise him in the heights.
Praise ye him, all his angels: praise ye him all his hosts.
Praise ye him, sun and moon: praise him, all ye stars
of light.
Praise him, ye heaven of heavens, and ye waters that be
above the heavens.
Let them praise the name of the Lord: for he
commanded and they were created.
He hath also established them for ever and ever:
he hath made a decree which shall not pass.
Praise the Lord from the earth, ye dragons, and all
ye deeps:
Fire, and hail; snow, and vapors; stormy wind fulfilling
his word:
Mountains, and all hills; fruitful trees, and all cedars;
Beasts, and all cattle; creeping things, and flying fowl:
Kings of the earth, and all people; princes, and all
judges of the earth;
Both young men, and maidens; old men and children:
Let them praise the name of the Lord: for his name
alone is excellent;
his glory is above the earth and heaven.
He also exalteth the horn of his people, the praise of
all his saints;
even the children of Israel, a people near unto him.
Praise ye the Lord.

  —Psalm 148

My soul doth magnify the Lord,

And my spirit hath rejoiced in God my Savior.

For he hath done great things for me, and holy is
   his name.

His mercy is upon them that fear him from generation
   to generation.

He hath showed the might of his arm; he hath scattered
   the proud in their conceit.

He hath put down the mighty from their thrones, and
   hath raised up the lowly.

He hath filled the hungry with good things, and the
   rich he hath sent empty away.

   —Luke 1:46-53, the prayer of Mary
      traditionally known as the "Magnificat"

Petition: Asking God for Things

If thanksgiving is one of the most natural forms of prayer to rise to our lips, then so is petition. All of us are needy creatures. Even if we are blessed by material abundance, we have emotional, spiritual, and physical requirements that need to be met every single day of our lives. And so we turn to others and to God to ask for things.

Of course, we don't always want what's best for us. Our motives are frequently mixed, and we may ask for something we don't need or shouldn't have. But throughout human history—no matter how secular society has become, no matter how mighty a culture has become—people have turned to God to ask for their needs to be met.

Children are the neediest of all, since they are dependent on grown-ups for almost everything. How easy it is for parents to become exhausted and irritated by their children's incessant clamoring for things. Toys. Snacks. Candy. Clothes. Outings to parks, movies, malls. Staying up at night for just another hour. Friends to sleep over. The keys to the car. How much of our time is spent saying, "No!" "Not yet!" "In your dreams!"

As parents, we want our children to learn self-restraint, to place their needs in the larger context of the family and the world. But there are also things that we hope they *will* ask for. We want them, for example, to know when to ask for help—from family, friends, teachers, and God—and when to turn outward and seek the good of others. We hope they will come to us when they are sad, afraid, or lonely, and find us to be willing listeners.

Here we touch on one of the central themes of the spiritual life: the need to purify our desires, to learn how to want what is best for us. The human heart is a restless thing, always ready to believe that if only it gets what it desires, happiness will be sure to follow. And yet most of us suspect that our heart, like an untended garden, will quickly become choked with weeds if we don't cultivate it. So we make New Year's resolutions or give things up for Lent or just vow to set our sights higher.

Prayer can help us cultivate our own hearts as well as those of our children. When we place our needs, hopes, and wishes before God, we are already beginning to put things into perspective. The very act of prayer asks us to step out of our subjective preoccupations for a time and set them against the higher values of faith, hope, and love. A child who asks for these gifts, and for God's blessings on the people he loves, near and far, will be less likely to fall into the self-absorption that is so common among young people today.

At the same time, prayer is not just about denying oneself; it also summons us to boldly offer up to God's mercy whatever is in our hearts. Children ought to know that nothing that troubles them is off limits in prayer. The Bible is full of stories about men and women who challenge, question, and even bargain with God.

One of the great Hasidic rabbis was asked by his disciples to explain a phrase from the Psalms in which King David says, "And I am prayer." The rabbi turned to his disciples and said, "It is as if a poor man, who has not eaten in three days and whose clothes are in rags, should appear before the king. Is there any need for him to say what he wants? That is how David faced God—he was the prayer."

To become transparent before God, to tear down the walls of fear and hurt—that is what authentic prayer requires of us. Children, with their characteristic candor and lack of self-consciousness, have little problem opening their hearts and asking God for what they need.

The single most challenging thing about petitionary prayer is not the asking but the more complicated process of waiting for an answer. A child does not come equipped with explanations about why God might not give what was asked for. That's where we as parents have to summon our courage and venture out into the realm of ad hoc theology. Though we may feel uncomfortable offering answers that sound hollow in our ears, it is important that we be willing to think out loud about these matters. The simplest explanation we can think of is that God's responses to our prayers are like the colors of a stoplight: sometimes God replies with green for "yes," sometimes with red for "no," and often with yellow, which means that we have to slow down and wait for the answer.

Another analogy that children understand instinctively is that of God as a parent, someone who loves us unconditionally and wants us to grow and flourish. A child can comprehend that God, like any parent, will sometimes refuse to give us what we ask for if it isn't what's best for us. On the other hand, God can also surprise us with presents we never expected to receive.

When a friend of ours, the folk singer Jan Krist, heard that we were writing this book, she wrote to us about her experiences in teaching her children to pray. One of her stories had to do with the problem of God's answers to prayer. "Some of my children's prayers were answered swiftly," Jan wrote, "but others went unanswered for years. My daughter Amon prayed every night for five years for God to give her a 'best friend.' We lived in the city and there were few children her age in our neighborhood. She went to a private school where most of the children came from more affluent families than ours and she didn't feel accepted there. Her prayers were not met until we moved to a new neighborhood and put her in a new school, where she found her best friend. She is 23 now and is quick to remind me these days about how slow God can be in his answers to our prayers."

Petitionary prayer, like any kind of prayer, does not consist merely of the specific things we ask for; the *process* of asking is just as important (if not more so) than what we ask for. Before God, we should all become like children—dependent and wayward at times, but willing and able to send up our requests, large and small, with the confidence that a loving heart is listening to us and responding in myriad ways.

God whose Name is Love, happy children we;
Listen to the hymn that we sing to thee.
Help us to be good, always kind and true,
In the games we play or the work we do.
Bless us every one singing here to thee,
God whose name is Love, loving may we be! Amen.
    —Florence Hoatson

Our Father who art in heaven,
Hallowed be thy name.
Thy kingdom come.
Thy will be done on earth, as it is in heaven.
Give us this day our daily bread.
And forgive us our trespasses, as we forgive those
    who trespass against us.
And lead us not into temptation, but deliver us
    from evil:
For thine is the kingdom, the power and the glory,
    for ever and ever. Amen.
    —Matthew 6:9–13

Ask and you shall receive.
    —John 16:24

Be Thou my Guardian and my Guide
And hear me when I call;
Let not my slippery footsteps slide
And hold me lest I fall.
And if I tempted am to sin,

And outward things are strong,
Do Thou, O Lord, keep watch within
And save my soul from wrong.
   —Isaac Williams

Stay with me, and then I shall begin to shine as Thou
   shinest so as to be a light to others.
   —John Henry Newman

Lord God Almighty, Shaper and Ruler of all creatures,
we pray for Thy great mercy to guide us to Thy will,
to make our minds steadfast, to strengthen us against
   temptation,
to put far from us all unrighteousness. Shield us
   against our foes,
seen and unseen, teach us so that we may inwardly
   love Thee
above all things with a clean mind and a clean body,
for Thou art our Maker and our Redeemer, our Trust
   and our Hope. Amen.
   —King Alfred the Great

O Christ,
tirelessly you seek out those who are looking for you
and who think that you are far away;
teach us, at every moment,
to place our spirits in your hands.
   —Brother Roger of Taize

O gracious and holy Father,
give us wisdom to perceive you,
intelligence to understand you,
diligence to seek you,
patience to wait for you,
a heart to meditate upon you,
and a life to proclaim you,
through the power of the Spirit
of our Lord Jesus Christ.
   —Saint Benedict

Help us so to know you that we may truly love you,
and so to love you that we may fully serve you,
whom to serve is perfect freedom;
through Jesus Christ our Lord.
   —Saint Augustine

Lord, you are my lover
My longing,
My flowing stream,
My sun,
And I am your reflection.
   —Mechtild of Magdeburg

I asked for strength that I might achieve;
I was made weak that I might learn humbly to obey.
I asked for health that I might do greater things;
I was given infirmity that I might do better things.
I asked for riches that I might be happy;
I was given poverty that I might be wise.
I asked for power that I might have the praise of men;
I was given weakness that I might feel the need of God.
I asked for all things that I might enjoy life;
I was given life that I might enjoy all things.
I got nothing that I had asked for,
but everything that I had hoped for.
Almost despite myself my unspoken prayers were
    answered;
I am, among all men, most richly blessed.
    —Prayer of an unknown Confederate soldier

You made me to find you; give me strength to seek you.
My strength and my weakness are in your hands:
preserve my strength and help my weakness.
Where you have opened the door, let me enter in;
where it is shut, open to my knocking.
Let me ever increase in remembering you,
understanding you, loving you,
until you restore me to your perfect pattern.
    —Saint Augustine

Seeking Forgiveness

When our children were small and we had had various altercations with them during the course of the day, we often found, on retiring for the night, little apology notes left on our beds. Some of them are priceless and are stored away in our special archive for such masterpieces. One of the best came in an elaborately decorated envelope that was covered with the "peace" sign, marked as "Sorry Mail!" and addressed to us at "323 South Bedroom, Sleepytown, PA 1934-bed." The letter of apology inside was accompanied by a special "Coupon Pack" that entitled us to a number of free services, including taking the baby "all day," helping Dad paint the house, and cleaning the bathrooms. Another favorite was addressed to "Dear Mummy." It reads: "I love you. I'm sorry I acted the way I did. Please forgive me. Send my love to Dad. P.S. I just couldn't sleep so I drew." The illustrated poem on the left-hand page reads: "Your as sweet as candy, as hip as a mummy [picture of Egyptian mummy], as bright as the sun, as cool as the breeze." Finally, a somewhat more earthy (and ambivalent) note, written after a dispute about the wearing of a pair of jeans, says: "Dear Mum, I'm sorry very much. I just don't like jeans. My legs aren't fit for jeans my legs get soar and tired. I'm very sorry about all this. It even gives me a wedgie. Worse than yours."

We treasure these notes not so much for their sense of humor (intended or unintended) as for what that humor signifies—that our children have an unshakable trust that we will forgive them. Though our family has its fair share of knock-down drag-out fights, grumpy outbursts, and recurrent skirmishes, it's comforting to know that we have done something to lay down a bedrock of forgiveness on which everyone unconsciously relies.

Because children haven't learned to disguise their emotions, it is often possible to see in their faces how deeply they long for the reunion that forgiveness brings. Still, it isn't easy for two people who feel aggrieved to find the humility to put aside their battle of wills and find reconciliation. That's why seeking forgiveness in prayer can be so essential to the peace and harmony of family life. There is an old religious saying that marriage involves three partners: the husband, the wife, and God. The meaning of the saying is simple: without the grace and love of God, a marriage can become little more than a battle of wills—a standoff without the hope of resolution. Given the high rate of divorce today, it's hard not to have some sympathy with the spirit of this old cliché.

The truth of this saying is proved every time a family prays together for forgiveness. When God is the unseen partner in prayer, the act of surrendering our pride becomes much easier. In the section on evening prayer, we discuss the tradition known as the "examination of conscience," in which we are to reflect on the day and confess any sins we have committed that day. In our family, this part of our nighttime prayer has provided many opportunities for apologies and reconciliations.

Theologians have often debated whether forgiving also means forgetting. Some scholars point out that forgiveness doesn't automatically blot out the memory, or the pain, of an offense. There's a great deal of truth to that, but it sounds to us like an adult truth. Children are less brittle and less interested in nurturing grudges: they really *do* tend to forget when they've been forgiven. May we all learn a little of that holy forgetfulness.

Sweet Jesus, ever watchful over me,
Let not my thoughts be evil,
Let not my words be wild,
Let not my acts be willful.
Watch the door of my lips
That I may tell no lie.
Grant me grace to guard my senses,
Strength to keep my temper,
Courage to deny myself. Amen.
—Father W. Roche, S.J.

Forgive us our trespasses, as we forgive those
who trespass against us.
    —Matthew 6:12

Lord, I am not worthy to receive You, but only say
the word and I shall be healed.
    —From the Liturgy of the Eucharist (Catholic)

Jesus Christ, have mercy on me,
As Thou art king of majesty;
And forgive my sins all
That I have done, both great and small;
And bring me, if it be Thy will
To heaven to dwell aye with Thee still.
    —Richard Rolle

O Almighty God, we humbly ask you to make us like
trees planted by the waterside, that we may bear fruits
of good living in due season. Forgive our past offenses,
sanctify us now, and direct all that we should be in the
future; for Christ's sake.
    —Prayer from Nigeria

O God, help us not to despise or oppose what we
do not understand.
    —William Penn

In your mercy, O my God,
save me from the proud,
and help me be not proud myself.

Deliver me from sin
and keep my tongue from doing wrong
by committing slander, speaking evil
and quarreling
with anyone at all.

   —Part of a text quoted in the Talmud

Our Father,
forgive all our misdeeds
and wipe away our sin,
for you are great and compassionate;
your mercy knows no bounds.
My heart lies before you, O my God.
Look deep within it.
See these memories of mine, for you are my hope.

   —Saint Augustine

Holy Spirit,
giving life to all life,
moving all creatures,
root of all things,
washing them clean,
wiping out their mistakes,
healing their wounds,
you are our true life,
luminous, wonderful,
awakening the heart
from its ancient sleep.

   —Hildegard of Bingen

From all blindness of heart, from pride, vainglory,
    and hypocrisy;
from envy, hatred, and malice, and all uncharitableness,
Good Lord, deliver us.
    —*Book of Common Prayer*

Amazing grace! how sweet the sound,
That saved a wretch like me!
I once was lost, but now am found,
Was blind, but now I see.
The Lord has promised good to me,
God's word my hope secures;
God will my shield and portion be
As long as life endures.
Through many dangers, toils and snares,
I have already come;
'Tis grace has brought me safe thus far,
And grace will lead me home.
    —John Newton

Loving God, our source of life,
you know our weakness.
May we reach out with joy to grasp your hand
and walk more readily in your ways.
    —*Catholic Household Blessings and Prayers*

Love bade me welcome: yet my soul drew
    back,
Guilty of dust and sin.
But quick-eyed Love, observing me grow slack
    From my first entrance in,

Drew nearer to me, sweetly questioning
    If I lacked any thing.
"A guest," I answered, "worthy to be here":
    Love said, "You shall be he."
"I the unkind, ungrateful? Ah, my dear,
    I cannot look on thee."
Love took my hand, and smiling did reply,
    "Who made the eyes but I?"
"Truth Lord, but I have marred them: let my
    shame
Go where it doth deserve."
"And know you not," says Love, "who bore
    the blame?"
"My dear, then I will serve."
"You must sit down," says Love, "and taste
    my meat":
So I did sit and eat.
    —George Herbert, "A Dialogue
      Between God and the Soul"

O Heavenly King, the Comforter, the Spirit of Truth
    who art everywhere and fillest all things.
Treasury of Blessings, and Giver of Life: Come and
    abide in us, and cleanse us from every impurity,
    and save our souls, O Good One.
O most-holy Trinity: have mercy on us.
O Lord: cleanse us from our sins.
O Master: pardon our transgressions.
O Holy One: visit and heal our infirmities, for
    Thy name's sake.
    —Saint John Chrysostom

I love you Jesus, my love, above all things;
I repent with my whole heart for having offended you.
Never permit me to separate myself from you again.
Grant that I may love you always then do with me
   what you will.
   —Stations of the Cross (Catholic)

God, give us grace to accept with serenity
the things that cannot be changed,
courage to change the things that should be changed,
and the wisdom to distinguish the one from the other.
   —Reinhold Niebuhr

Silent Prayer and Meditation

A t first glance, you might think that the notion of putting the words *silence* and *children* in the same sentence is hysterically funny. And we'd have to concede that you may have a point. Once we tried to encourage our older kids (then aged ten, twelve, and fourteen) to observe a period of silence before we said evening prayers as a way of quieting down their thoughts and preparing to enter into a spirit of prayerfulness. For at least five minutes, we tried, without success, to stop the kids from breaking the silence with questions, giggles, and wiseacre comments. Then, when silence had descended for all of thirty seconds, one of the kids made a loud noise—which, out of courtesy, we will not describe for you, dear reader. (Suffice it to say that it was what Suzanne calls one of the "sins of emission.") Suddenly all of us were rolling on the floor, laughing hysterically.

So much for our first experiment in silent prayer.

Nonetheless, we have persisted with our attempts to practice silence and have achieved a modest amount of success (more on that in a moment). But why should we even bother with silent prayer? It might seem more likely that rivers will flow uphill before kids manage to be quiet for more than a few seconds at a time.

But silence and prayer are intimately linked, and any attempt to pray without a grounding in quietness will never amount to much. Our friend Leah Buturain shared with us something that she explains to her children. Leah reminds them that if we forget to be quiet and listen, that is tantamount to calling someone on the phone, talking away, and then hanging up before the person has a chance to respond. We listen to those we love in silence.

We need silence to quiet our restless thoughts and anxieties, the constant temptation to always worry about the future and not dwell peacefully in the present moment. Not only does silence help us know our own hearts better, but it also puts us in a better position to hear God's still, small voice. Against the backdrop of silence, our words are more measured; they emerge from our lips with more meaning and dignity.

Children *are* capable of being silent. When they are absorbed in some new experience, whether they are encountering a wonder of nature or learning something that fascinates them, they can become extremely still, like a radar dish turned to receive a signal from a particular direction. At these moments, they can take in vast amounts of knowledge and experience. (A refreshing change from radio, television, computers, stereos, movie theaters, Muzak piped in over the shopping mall's P.A. system, boomboxes, and portable media players with headphones—the wall of sound, news, and information that surrounds us with a constant drone.)

There are many ways to try to introduce a little healing silence into your children's lives, including silent reading and outdoor walks. (Greg tries to get our kids to be silent when they're out stargazing, with at least occasional success.) Silent prayer is another option. Praying in silence allows us to cultivate a sense of intimacy with God; it can consist of words said in the mind or in wordless meditation and wonder.

Silent prayer can be a part of your family prayer time, or it can be something you and your kids practice on your own. We occasionally preface our family evening prayers with a minute or so of silence and have found it to be an effective method for making the transition from our busy, distracted selves to our more meditative selves.

We've also begun to experiment with icons and other classic works of art as a focal point for silent meditation. Children and adults alike often find that an image can provide the necessary gateway into a deeper state of consciousness. Depending on your own personal beliefs and tastes, you might find that a painting of a biblical scene, a saint, or a heroic person or even a photograph of natural beauty may be conducive to silent meditation.

Of course, the following prayers require us to speak (even in our minds). But they summon us to a deeper relationship with silence. Saint Francis always began his prayers with the sentence "Let us place ourselves in God's presence." Many of these prayers can be said immediately before a period of silent prayer is observed.

There are other prayers that resonate well with silence. An example can be found in the first prayer of this section, often called the "Jesus Prayer." Traditionally, this prayer is said many times so that it may become a gateway to the contemplation of God's love. Another approach might be to say this prayer less frequently, repeating it only when our minds begin to wander too far from God.

⌒

Lord Jesus Christ, son of God, have mercy on me,
a sinner.
    —Ancient Christian prayer known as
      the "Jesus Prayer"

Christ be with me, Christ be within me,
Christ behind me, Christ before me,
Christ beside me, Christ to win me,
Christ to comfort and restore me.
Christ beneath me, Christ above me,
Christ in quiet, Christ in danger,
Christ in hearts of all who love me,
Christ in mouth of friend or stranger.
    —From the prayer known as the
      "Breastplate of Saint Patrick"

Like weary waves,
thought flows upon thought,
but the still depth beneath
is all thine own.
   —George Macdonald

Teach me the power and the strength of silence,
that I may go into the world
as still as a mouse
in the depths of my heart.
   —After Mechtild of Magdeburg

Drop thy still dews of quietness,
Till all our strivings cease;
Take from our souls the strain and stress,
And let our ordered lives confess
The beauty of thy peace.
   —John Greenleaf Whittier

Let me seek you in my desire,
Let me desire you in my seeking.
Let me find you by loving you
Let me love you when I find you.
   —Saint Anselm

Lord, teach me to seek you,
and reveal yourself to me as I look for you.
For I cannot seek you unless first you teach me,
nor find you unless first you reveal yourself to me.
   —Saint Ambrose

Take, Lord, all my liberty,
my memory, my understanding,
and my whole will.
You have given me all that I have,
all that I am,
and I surrender all to Your Divine Will.
You have given me all that I have,
all that I am,
and I surrender all to Your Divine Will.
Give me only Your love and Your grace.
With this I am rich enough,
and I have no more to ask.
Amen.
—Saint Ignatius of Loyola

Govern everything by your wisdom, O Lord, so that my
soul may always be serving you
in the way you will
and not as I choose.
Let me die to myself so that I may serve you;
let me live to you who are life itself.
Amen.
—Saint Teresa of Avila

We were enclosed,
O eternal Father,
within the garden of your breast.
You drew us out of your holy mind like a flower
petaled with our soul's three powers,
and into each power you put the whole plant,
so that they might bear fruit in your garden,
might come back to you with the fruit you gave them.
And you would come back to the soul,
to fill her with your blessedness.
There the soul dwells—
like the fish in the sea
and the sea in the fish.

 —Saint Catherine of Siena

Short-Attention-Span Prayers (SASPs)

We owe this slightly facetious phrase to our friend William Griffin, a Christian writer who has the ability to make everyone around him burst into fits of laughter. Though he often writes about spiritual things, Bill's feet are always planted on terra firma; he's what you might call a "spiritual realist." When Bill gave a brief talk on short-attention-span prayers (or SASPs, as he called them), he pointed out that Catholics used to call these brief, one-line prayers *ejaculations*. It's not a word, he noted with a twinkle in his eye, that we tend to associate with prayer these days.

But Bill Griffin had a practical, down-to-earth point to make, and it's simply this: most of us lead busy lives and are either too distracted or too preoccupied to set aside much time for prayer. And though we like to think of our children as having lots of free time, the truth is that school, home-work, sports, lessons, summer camp, and all the other activi-ties kids participate in nowadays have made their lives more rushed and harried than we parents would like to admit. It's all too easy to be caught up in the daily grind and lose any sense of connection to the sacred.

Many religious traditions encourage their followers to say brief prayers—often a single sentence or just a phrase—at var-ious times and for various occasions. Most of the daily emo-tions and experiences we have can become the occasion for prayer. A beautiful sunny day might evoke in us a passing feeling of gratitude. To give that feeling some depth or reso-nance, to celebrate it more vividly, we can offer up a brief prayer: "Thanks be to God!" Far from being merely senti-mental or cute, such prayers enable us to live in a heightened state of awareness of God's presence and love.

From a child's perspective, there are many times when the comfort of prayer offers strength and peace. When we're afraid, as a child might be before taking a test, going to the doctor or dentist, or dealing with the emotional highs and lows of social life, a prayer for protection and grace can settle our beating heart. Fear, anger, insecurity—these and similar emotions sometimes lead us to get too caught up in the mo-ment, unable to step back and see the bigger picture. A short prayer, though it can't solve all our problems or make them go away, can help us calm down and take stock of our situa-tion. When we're under stress, we often break the tension through some form of violence, even if that violence is only a harsh word.

It might be objected that these short one-line prayers could degenerate into something akin to superstition, as if they were charms or amulets to ward off evil spirits. This is a legitimate concern. Any good thing has its potential abuse, and the ever-present danger with prayer is that it becomes merely rote, a muttered formula rather than a cry from the heart.

However, we think that such short prayers, if they are suggested to children in the right spirit, ought to be no different than any other type of prayer: shouts of praise or calls for help. Some of the short prayers we present here are classics, but there is no reason why you and your children shouldn't use the words that rise spontaneously to your lips.

Saint Paul admonished his fellow believers to "pray without ceasing"; in a similar vein, the Talmud directs observant Jews to say one hundred blessings every day. These are just two of the lofty pronouncements one encounters when reading the spiritual masters; they're the kinds of sayings that can stop us in our tracks and make us blink in stunned disbelief. Who, aside from contemplative monks on mountaintops or in hushed cloisters, can possibly be expected to pray all the time? But as Bill Griffin reminds us, even the most distracted and preoccupied person can find many moments in the day to fire off a prayer. We'd venture to say that these simple bursts of prayer, emerging as they do out of the chaos and distractions of our days, help us cultivate the spirit of devotion of which the masters speak.

Thanks be to God.

Glory to God in the highest.

Alleluia!

Lord, stay with me.

Thy will be done.

Help me, Lord.

The Lord is my shepherd, I shall not want.
   —Psalm 23:1

Blessed are you, Lord God, ruler of the universe.

Blessed is the person who comes in the name
of the Lord.

Lord, I am not worthy, but only say the word and
I shall be healed.

Lamb of God, who takes away the sins of the world,
grant me peace.

Lord, I believe. Help thou my unbelief.
   —Mark 9:24

Lord, make me a channel of your peace.
   —Saint Francis

This is the day the Lord has made. Let us rejoice
and be glad in it.
   —Psalm 118:24

Prayers for Parents, Grandparents, and All Who Love Children

Throughout this book, we've stressed that praying with your children can become the springboard that can help you develop your own prayer life. That's why we think it is important to not only pray *with* your children but also to pray *for* them—on your own. If you do not pray on a regular basis, praying for your children can become the bridge to new habits, new patterns of spiritual awareness.

As much as we love our children, we're harried, fallible people who need to take time to reflect on the needs of these precious gifts. In the peace of prayer, we have the opportunity to make explicit things that have been niggling at the backs of our minds. In prayer, we can make resolutions to do better and ask for the strength to carry out those resolutions.

Also, children, with their finely tuned spiritual sensor systems, *know* that you are praying for them. In his memoir *Christ the Tiger,* Thomas Howard writes of his devout Protestant father, who would get up at dawn and pray for his family and a host of others held dear, from local friends to far-flung missions around the globe. When Thomas came down for breakfast, his father would still be on his knees, and the feeling of his love would enfold him.

Few of us have the time and energy (and, let's face it, *devotion*) of Thomas Howard's father, but we can nevertheless set aside time to pray for our kids. We're not suggesting that you do so in some obvious way, as if to show off what you're doing; kids just *know.*

Of course, the circle of prayer need not be restricted to the nuclear family of parents and children. Members of the extended family—grandparents, aunts, and uncles—have played vital roles in the moral and spiritual growth of children throughout the ages.

There are times when the *only* people praying for a child come from the extended family, because the child's parents don't pray. Should you let your grandchildren, nieces, or nephews know that you are praying for them or even perhaps pray *with* them? These are obviously delicate matters that can only be addressed in specific contexts and with great prudence and tact. If prayer truly has an impact on the world, as we believe it does, then the grace it brings will become manifest in many quiet, unobtrusive ways.

The words of the prayers presented here, as elsewhere in the book, can be adapted to fit your relationship with the children you are praying for.

Then hear thou from heaven thy dwelling place,
and forgive, and render unto every man according
unto all his ways, whose heart thou knowest; (for
thou only knowest the hearts of the children of men).
That they may fear thee, to walk in thy ways, so long
as they live in the land.
　　—2 Chronicles 6:30-31

Lord our God, you watch over us with the anxious
care of a mother and the protective pride of a father;
help us not only nurture the spiritual lives of our
children but also learn from their innocence, wonder,
and trust, so that we may grow together as a family
united in your love. Amen.
　　—Gregory Wolfe

Prayer of a Single Parent

My Lord and Holy Companion,
I am alone in the awesome task of making a home.
I ask Your holy help
to show me how to take on the responsibilities
of both mother and father.
Direct my heart
so that I may dispense the qualities of both parents,
of gentle compassion on one hand,
of firm discipline on the other;
may I transmit true tenderness coupled with true
　　strength.

These twin talents of the masculine and feminine
are both within me,
but it is difficult, Lord,
to balance their daily expression in our home.
The days are long and the nights lonely,
yet, with Your divine support,
the impossible will unfold as possible,
and our home will be more than a house.
My efforts to be two persons
find my time directed to a great degree
toward the needs of others;
yet I, as well, am in need of comfort and love.
Let my prayer,
my Lord and Secret One,
renew my energy
and remind me that I am not alone.
For you, my Lord, are with me!
The pathway of tomorrow is hidden from me;
perhaps it is just as well.
May the unknown future
only cast me into deeper trust and love of You
and fill my heart
with love enough for two. Amen.

   —Edward Hays

O Lord my God, shed the light of your love on my
child. Keep her safe from all illness and injury. Enter
her tiny soul, and comfort her with your peace and joy.
She is too young to speak to me, and to my ears her
cries and gurgles are meaningless nonsense. But to
your ears they are prayers. Her cries are cries for your
blessing. Her gurgles are of delight at your grace. Let
her as a child learn the way of your commandments.
As an adult let her live the full span of life, serving
your kingdom on earth. And finally in her old age
let her die in the sure and certain knowledge of your
salvation. I do not ask that she be wealthy, powerful,
or famous. Rather I ask that she be poor in spirit,
humble in action, and devout in worship. Dear Lord,
smile upon her.

    —After Johann Starck

Starting forth on life's rough way,
Father, guide them;
O! We know not what of harm
May betide them;
'Neath the shadow of Thy wing,
Father, hide them;
Waking, sleeping, Lord, we pray,
God beside them.
When in prayer they cry to Thee,
Do Thou hear them;
From the stains of sin and shame
Do Thou clear them;
'Mid the quicksands and the rocks,

Do Thou steer them;
In Temptation, trial, grief,
Be Thou near them.
Unto Thee we give them up,
Lord, receive them;
In the world we know must be
Much to grieve them—
Many striving oft and strong
To deceive them.
Trustful in Thy hands of love
We must leave them.

    —William Cullen Bryant, "A Mother's Prayer"

The Spirit of Service

P rayer has been called "love in action," but authentic prayer impels us to move into the realm of deeds. As the spiritual writer Richard Foster has put it, "To pray is to change." This change will inevitably cause us to seek to bring constructive change to the world around us. And that, it seems to us, is the basis for service. One of the twentieth-century's greatest servants, Martin Luther King Jr., once said, "Everybody can be great. Because anybody can serve. You don't have to have a college degree to serve. You don't have to make your subject and your verb agree to serve. You don't have to know about Plato and Aristotle to serve. You don't have to know Einstein's theory of relativity to serve. You only need a heart full of grace. A soul generated by love."

At the national summit on volunteerism that took place in 1997, leaders from all walks of life called on Americans to achieve a new commitment to service. Indeed, various organizations and governmental agencies have been working hard to instill a willingness to serve in our young people, perhaps as an antidote to the selfishness of our consumerist society.

The issue of service is a knotty one for our family, one that we often struggle with. As full-time writers, we find it almost impossible to consider any of our time truly "free," since we are constantly working under the pressure of deadlines. With four children to raise, it just isn't possible for us to devote ourselves to the many worthwhile volunteer projects being undertaken in our community. We also don't have much, in a monetary sense, to give away to good causes. But despite all these fine excuses, our consciences nag us: Are we really doing as much as we can to serve others?

What we *have* tried to do, from time to time, is offer our home to individuals who are going through difficult times—more often than not, times of emotional distress and painful transition. Though it is always a challenge to fit another adult into our home and its routines, we've found ways to make room for an "extended family."

It would be wrong to depict these efforts at hospitality as totally stress-free. After all, our guests have often had to work through a lot of anguish and uncertainty. We've learned that if you respond to the biblical injunction that we "bear one another's burdens," you have to be prepared for a process that can be messy and uncomfortable as well as joyful and healing.

The most startling revelation that has emerged from these episodes with visitors has to do with our children.

When we began to bring people into our home, we worried about the potential impact on the kids. Would they be *too* burdened by these invasions of their privacy? As it turns out, we shouldn't have worried. Children who receive love themselves have an astonishingly acute intuition about the emotional needs of others, and they can express love in ways that provide balm to the most haggard of souls. It's not just that playing with children has therapeutic value for people in distress. There's more to it than that. Children have remarkable powers of empathy and can fine-tune their responses to the people around them. They also have the ability to demonstrate unconditional love.

Our kids have adopted every one of our guests, treating them as honorary aunts and uncles. In this sense, they've learned that the ultimate meaning of service grows out of direct relationships, the concrete experience of one person helping another, rather than abstract idealism. And they incorporate these visitors into their prayers. Watching them render this sort of service has filled us with awe and a great deal of pride. It's not hard to imagine these children bringing the same spirit to any form of service we might ask of them.

As we noted earlier in this book, there are innumerable opportunities to link prayer with service to society. Whether it is volunteering in a soup kitchen, visiting the elderly, or holding a fundraising event in your community for a worthy cause, there are tremendous emotional and spiritual rewards when families render service together.

How shall I not give you all that I have,
when you, in your great goodness, give me all that
    you are?
    —Anonymous

Dearest Lord, teach me to be generous.
Teach me to serve You as You deserve;
To give and not to count the cost;
To fight and not to heed the wounds;
To toil and not to seek reward,
Save that of knowing that
I do Your will, O God.
    —Saint Ignatius of Loyola

Christ has no body now on earth but yours;
yours are the only hands with which he can do
    his work,
yours are the only feet with which he can go about
    the world,
yours are the only eyes through which his compassion
can shine forth upon a troubled world.
Christ has no body on earth now but yours.
    —Saint Teresa of Avila

O Lord our God, give us by thy Holy Spirit
a willing heart and a ready hand
to use all thy gifts to thy praise and glory;
through Jesus Christ our Lord.
    —Archbishop Cranmer

Heavenly Father, whose blessed Son came not to be served but to serve: Bless all who, following in his steps, give themselves to the service of others; that with wisdom, patience, and courage, they may minister in his Name to the suffering, the friendless, and the needy; for the love of him who laid down his life for us, your Son our Savior Jesus Christ, who lives and reigns with you and the Holy Spirit, one God, for ever and ever. Amen.

    —*Book of Common Prayer*

Peace and Justice

Whenever adults get together to discuss such large-scale
social problems as drug use, violence, and teenage
pregnancy, one solution that is nearly always put forward is
that of "better education." If only our children hear the correct messages from an early age, the reasoning goes, they
won't make such costly and tragic mistakes. And yet even
where such educational programs have been in place for
years, the problems persist—and often get worse.

In attempting to account for the failure of such efforts, a
growing number of parents and educators have come to the
conclusion that they were based on false premises. The notion that children only need the right information—and perhaps some strong exhortations to "just say no"—to make the
right choices in life is now regarded by many as sentimental

and dangerously naïve. Indeed, new research has bolstered a rather old-fashioned idea: that children need to internalize the habits and disciplines of the moral life in the home if they are to have the capacity to say no to bad things and actively embrace the good. The facts, messages, and exhortations conveyed at school tend to remain abstract because they are addressed primarily to the head. But in the daily struggle in which family members must make sacrifices, tolerate differences, and accept responsibilities—these everyday habits give shape and form to the heart.

The spiritual truth that we ignore at our peril is our dependence on one another. The attempt to deny our interdependence is the cause of all our woes. When Adam and Eve break faith with God and try to live on their own, selfishness and discord replace the peace of Eden.

Prayer is the means by which we seek to regain our connectedness to God and to our neighbors. Prayer employs a language of the heart that is at once more intimate and more concrete than the often windy rhetoric of politics. It also provides a contemplative space that can serve as the seedbed for authentic social action.

Ultimately, peace and justice are rooted in compassion for our neighbors, in a transcendent love that restores the web of human interdependence. Since the first neighbors we encounter in life are our own family members, it's not hard to see why someone once said that charity begins at home.

In their book *Parenting for Peace and Justice,* Kathleen and James McGinnis suggest that children be encouraged to clip an article from the newspaper and incorporate it into a family "litany" wherein each family member shares a story that is either distressing or hopeful. Then the family prays for the situation mentioned in the story. The rest of the family can respond with a phrase like "Lord, hear my prayer." Whether the stories come from the newspaper or from the TV evening news, we think the McGinnises have a good idea, one that would apply to any of the themes in this book.

⌒

Blessed are the peacemakers: for they shall be
called the children of God.
    —Matthew 5:9

Blessed are they which do hunger and thirst after
    righteousness: for they shall be filled.
    —Matthew 5:10

Lord, make me an instrument of your peace.
Where there is hatred, let me sow love,
Where there is injury, pardon;
Where there is doubt, faith;
Where there is despair, hope;
Where there is darkness, light;
And where there is sadness, joy.
O, Divine Master, grant that I may not so much
seek to be consoled as to console,
to be understood as to understand,
to be loved as to love.
For it is in giving that we receive,
it is in pardoning that we are pardoned,
and it is in dying that we are born to eternal life.
    —Saint Francis

O God, the Lord of all,
your Son commanded us to love our enemies
and to pray for them.
Lead us from prejudice to truth;
deliver us from hatred, cruelty, and revenge;
and enable us to stand before you,
reconciled through your Son, Jesus Christ our Lord.
 Amen.
 —*Catholic Household Blessings and Prayers*

The peace of God
which passes all understanding,
keep our hearts and minds
in the knowledge and love of Jesus Christ our Lord;
and the blessing of God Almighty,
the Father, the Son and the Holy Spirit,
be upon us and remain with us always.
 —Adapted from Philippians 4:7

O Lord Jesus, stretch forth your wounded hands in
blessing over your people, to heal and restore, and
to draw them to yourself and to one another in love.
 —Prayer from the Middle East (slightly amended
  and modernized)

Peace between neighbors,
Peace between kindred,
Peace between lovers,
In the love of the King of life.
Peace between person and person,
Peace between wife and husband,
Peace between women and children,

The peace of Christ above all peace.
Bless, O Christ, my face.
Let my face bless everything;
Bless, O Christ, mine eye,
Let mine eye bless all it sees.
　　—Traditional Gaelic prayer

Lord our God, who created the rainbow to remind us
that all colors are contained in the radiance of your
divine light, help us overcome our fears and prejudices
and learn to see your face in the cultures and peoples
of the world, so that we might deepen our compassion
and expand our knowledge of the human heart, through
your Son, Jesus Christ.
　　—Gregory Wolfe

God our Father, Creator of the world,
please help us love one another.
Make nations friendly with other nations;
make all of us love one another like a family.
Help us do our part to bring peace in the world
and happiness to all people.
　　—Prayer from Japan

Almighty God, ever-loving Father,
your care extends beyond the boundaries of race
　　and nation
to the hearts of all who live.
May the walls, which prejudice raises between us,
crumble beneath the shadow of your outstretched arm.
We ask through Christ our Lord.
　　—*Liturgy of the Hours*

We thank you, Lord, that we are citizens of a world made up of different races. Your grace touches us all, whatever our race and color. We rejoice in the richness of our cultures, our music and dance, our folklore and legends. We thank you for all these gifts. We delight in the joy they bring to our lives.

—Adapted from *Women of Brazil*

Save me, O Lord, from selfishness—especially when I am saying my prayers. When I ask something for myself, may I remember all the others who want it as well, and never let me forget the boys and girls of other lands as well as at home who are hungry and lonely and unhappy. So I pray now: God bless all children everywhere.

—Donald O. Soper

Blessed are the poor in spirit: for theirs is the kingdom of heaven.

—Matthew 5:3

Praise the Lord! Praise, O servants of the Lord; praise
    the name of the Lord.
Blessed be the name of the Lord from this time on
    and forevermore.
He raises the poor from the dust, and lifts the needy
    from the ash heap,
to make them sit with princes, with the princes of
    his people.

—Psalm 113:1-2, 7-8

God, our sustainer,
You have called out your people into
the wilderness
to travel your unknown ways.
Make us strong to leave behind false
security and comfort,
and give us new hope in our calling;
that the desert may blossom as a
rose,
and your promises may be fulfilled in us.
In the name of Jesus Christ. Amen.
    —Janet Morley

Faith of our fathers, living still
In spite of dungeon, fire and sword,
O how our hearts beat high with joy
Whene'er we hear that glorious word!
Faith of our fathers, holy faith,
We will be true to thee till death.
Our fathers, chained in prisons dark,
Were still in heart and conscience free,
And blest would be their children's fate,
Though they, like him, should die for thee.
Faith of our fathers, holy faith,
We will be true to thee till death.
Faith of our fathers, faith and prayer,
Shall keep our country brave and free,
And through the truth that comes from God,
Our land shall then indeed be free.
Faith of our fathers, holy faith,
We will be true to thee till death.

Faith of our fathers, we will love
Both friend and foe in all our strife,
And preach thee, too, as love knows how
By kindly words and virtuous life.
Faith of our fathers, holy faith,
We will be true to thee till death.
　　　—Frederick W. Faber

O Brother Jesus, who as a child was carried into exile,
Remember all those who are deprived of their home
　　or country,
Who groan under the burden of anguish and sorrow,
Enduring the burning heat of the sun,
The freezing cold of the sea, or the humid heat of
　　the forest,
Searching for a place of refuge.
Cause these storms to cease, O Christ.
Move the hearts of those in power
That they may respect the men and women
Whom you have created in your own image;
That the grief of refugees may be turned into joy.
　　　—African prayer for refugees

O God of earth and altar,
Bow down and hear our cry;
Our earthly rulers falter,
Our people drift and die;
The walls of gold entomb us,
The swords of scorn divide;
Take not thy thunder from us,
But take away our pride.

From all that terror teaches,
From lies of tongue and pen,
From all the easy speeches
That comfort cruel men,
From sale and profanation
Of honor and the sword,
From sleep and from damnation,
Deliver us, good Lord.
　　—G. K. Chesterton

Have mercy, O God,
on all who are sorrowful,
those who weep and those in exile.
Have pity on the persecuted and the homeless
who are without hope;
those who are scattered
in remote corners of this world;
those who are in prison
and ruled by tyrants.
Have mercy on them
as is written in your holy law,
where your compassion
is exalted!
　　—Jewish prayer

I will extol thee, O Lord; for thou hast lifted me up,
and hast not made my foes to rejoice over me.
O Lord my God, I cried unto thee, and thou hast
healed me.
O Lord, thou hast brought up my soul from the grave:
thou hast kept me alive, that I should not go down
into the pit.
Sing unto the Lord, O ye saints of his, and give thanks
at the remembrance of his holiness.
For his anger endureth but a moment; in his favor is
life: weeping may endure for a night, but joy cometh
in the morning.

—Psalm 30:1-5

The Environment

One of the best family vacations we ever had was a two-week holiday on an island off the coast of Maine. Even though the island was barely a quarter of a mile from the mainland, it was still quite an adventure for landlubbers like us. Living in a small cottage only a few feet away from the water's edge, we were the sole possessors of the island, which is a little over thirty acres in size.

Very quickly we realized that this island could be seen as a microcosm: humanity and nature existed in a delicate balance. Little things could mar the beauty and pristine freshness of the place. Some previous (and obviously irresponsible) occupants of the cottage, for example, had broken some bottles on the beach, so our kids had to have shoes on at all times. We had to tell our son Charles to not dump huge globs of mud right beside a lobster pot near the shore. We would even find ourselves almost physically recoiling every time we'd see some trash floating in the water. It only took a few days for our children to learn new rules of respect—and even reverence—for the environment.

Over the past thirty years, we have become more concerned with the health of the environment than ever before. But in this same period, we have continued to place greater and greater strains on the natural world from which we spring.

Many Christians have turned to Native American lore to gain a deeper reverence for the natural realm. Native Americans have always had an intuitive understanding of the interdependence of all living things. Perhaps Chief Seattle of the Suquamish tribe put it most succinctly when he said, "This we know. The earth does not belong to man; man belongs to the earth. This we know. All things are connected. Whatever befalls the earth befalls the sons of the earth. Man did not weave the web of life. He is merely a strand in it. Whatever he does to the web, he does to himself."

The Judeo-Christian tradition, on the other hand, has come in for heavy criticism by certain environmental activists for allegedly fostering a view of humanity as the rapacious conqueror of nature. In the story of the Garden of Eden, the Bible speaks of humanity as having "dominion" over the created order, and there's little doubt that some arrogant souls in Western history have taken that to mean "domination." But the real meaning of the word *dominion* is closer to what we call stewardship, the solemn responsibility of caring for the natural world.

Children need no encouragement to revel in the beauty and grandeur of nature. With every hop, skip, and jump across a backyard or park, they pronounce their benediction on the goodness of creation.

God who made the earth, the air, the sky, the sea,
Who gave the light its birth, careth for me.
God who made the grass, the flower, the fruit, the tree,
The day and night to pass, careth for me.
God who made the sun, the moon, the stars,
is he who, when life's clouds come on, careth for me.
    —Anonymous

Refrain: All things bright and beautiful,
All creatures great and small,
All things wise and wonderful,
The Lord God made them all.

Each little flower that opens,
Each little bird that sings,
He made their glowing colors,
He made their tiny wings.
(*Refrain*)

The purple-headed mountain,
The river running by,
The sunset, and the morning
That brightens up the sky.
(*Refrain*)

The cold wind in the winter,
The pleasant summer sun,
The ripe fruits in the garden,
He made them ev'ry one.
(*Refrain*)

He gave us eyes to see them,
And lips that we might tell
How great is God Almighty,
Who has made all things well.
(*Refrain*)

   —Cecil Alexander

Praised be our Lord for the wind and the rain,
For clouds, for dew and the air;
For the rainbow set in the sky above
Most precious and kind and fair.
For all these things tell the love of our Lord,
The love that is everywhere.

   —Elizabeth Goudge

Most high, most powerful, good Lord, to you belong praise, glory, honor and all blessing!

Praised be my Lord God with all his creatures, and especially our brother the sun, who brings us the day and brings us the light; fair is he and shines with a great splendor.

O Lord, he signifies you.

Praised be my Lord for our sister the moon, and for the stars, which he has set clear and lovely in the heavens.

Praised be my Lord for our brother the wind, and for air and cloud, calms and all weather, by which you uphold life in all creatures.

Praised be my Lord for our sister water, who is very serviceable unto us and humble and precious and pure.

Praised be my Lord for our brother fire, through whom you give light in the darkness; and he is bright and pleasant and very mighty and strong.

Praised be my Lord for our mother the earth, who sustains us and keeps us, and brings forth various fruits and flowers of many colors.

Praise and bless the Lord, and give thanks to him, and serve him with great humility.
　　—Saint Francis

The earth is full of your goodness,
your greatness and understanding,
your wisdom and harmony.
How wonderful
are the lights that you created.
You formed them
with love, knowledge and understanding.
You endowed them
with strength and power,
and they shine very wonderfully on the world,
magnificent in their splendor.
They arise in radiance
and go down in joy.
Reverently

they fulfill your divine will.
They are tributes to your name
as they exalt your sovereign rule
in song.
    —Hymn probably composed by mystics
        at the time of the Second Temple

Be a gardener.
Dig a ditch,
toil and sweat,
and turn the earth upside down
and seek the deepness
and water the plants in time.
Continue this labor
and make sweet floods to run
and noble and abundant fruits to spring.
Take this food and drink
and carry it to God
as your true worship.
    —Julian of Norwich

The world is charged with the grandeur of God.
And for all this, nature is never spent;
    There lives the dearest freshness deep
    down things;
And though the last lights off the black
    West went
    Oh, morning, at the brown brink
    eastward, springs—
Because the Holy Ghost over the bent
    World broods with warm breast and
    with ah! bright wings.
    —Gerard Manley Hopkins

ACKNOWLEDGMENTS

We're grateful to a host of people who have helped us along the way.

Special thanks go to our agent, Carol Mann, for her support, and to our editor, Julianna Gustafson, for her insight and encouragement.

We have benefited enormously from conversations about prayer with Kim Alexander, Robert Atwan, Leah Buturain, Scott Cairns, David Cullen, Richard Foster, Emilie and William Griffin, Jan Krist, Madeleine L'Engle, Paul Mariani, Michael Medved, Kathleen Norris, Eugene Peterson, Luci Shaw, Jeanne Murray Walker, and Walter Wangerin Jr. We're grateful to all of them.

Our initial research and writing about family prayer was supported by a grant from the John Templeton Foundation.

Our children—Magdalen, Helena, Charles, and Benedict—have been our best teachers and guides in the life of prayer. They are living proof that prayer doesn't have to make one prissy or stuck up. Not by a long shot!

Finally, to the Three-in-One—Father, Son, and Holy Spirit—who hears all prayers—from stuttered pleas for help to the adoration of the mystics—with equal attention, and whose love sustains the universe, be all honor, glory, and praise, now and forever.

G.W. AND S.M.W.

THE AUTHORS

GREGORY WOLFE is Writer in Residence at Seattle Pacific University and the founder and editor of *Image: A Journal of the Arts and Religion,* one of America's leading literary quarterlies. Among his books are *Intruding Upon the Timeless: Meditations on Art, Faith, and Mystery; Malcolm Muggeridge: A Biography;* and *Sacred Passion: The Art of William Schickel.* Wolfe is also the editor of *The New Religious Humanists: A Reader* and the coauthor of *Books That Build Character.*

SUZANNE M. WOLFE recently published her first novel, *Unveiling.* She is also the coauthor of *Books That Build Character, The Family New Media Guide,* and *Climb High, Climb Far.* A professor of English literature at Seattle Pacific University, she has served for many years as the executive editor of *Image: A Journal of the Arts and Religion.*

GREGORY AND SUZANNE WOLFE live in Seattle with their four children.

CREDITS